Love and Forgiveness

A Pathway to Freedom

Ruth Hostak

WestBow Press books may be ordered through booksellers or by contacting:

WestBow Press
A Division of Thomas Nelson & Zondervan
1663 Liberty Drive
Bloomington, IN 47403
www.westbowpress.com
844-714-3454

ruthderm@aol.com

ISBN: 979-8-3850-0137-8 (sc)
ISBN: 979-8-3850-0138-5 (hc)
ISBN: 979-8-3850-0136-1 (e)

Library of Congress Control Number: 2023911508

Print information available on the last page.

WestBow Press rev. date: 7/28/2023

Dedication

I dedicate this memoir to the women in the Family of Women. For over thirty years you have empowered me to live my dreams and to reach my goals.

To my friends in the Wisdom Group who always encourages me to be the best version of myself.

To my friends in the Miracles Course, especially Carolina and Alice who inspire me every week.

The Holy Wisdom Parish where I worship. I get filled with the love of God each and every week.

I thank you all for being in my life and encouraging me to make a difference in the world.

Acknowledgements

I am forever grateful to the people in my life who have contributed to turning my dream into reality.

My husband Dan Hostak who always believed in me, encouraged me and stood by my side throughout the entire process. I love you with all my heart.

Ellen Gold who was the first person to encourage me to write my memoir. Thank you for your inspiration.

My writing coach Suzanne Lieurance who taught me the basics and did my first edit. She was encouraging and supportive. She gave me concrete suggestions and I took her advice.

My dear friend Paris Heart thank you for your love and commitment. You gave your best to assist me and I deeply appreciate it.

Thank you, Len and Linda for your kind words and your support of me.

Josephine Corcoran, you made a difference with the suggestions you gave me in having my work shine.

To my close friends who inspired me and rooted for me all along the way. Lesley-Rosenthal-Buchheim, Joan Dacken, Pat McKenna, Tony and Joe Malara. Jacqui Stevens.

Christina Craig and Joy Mastrocola thank you for your love and support along the way.

My friends in my weekly movie group who I have been participating with for many years in the Family of Women, Circle of Hearts, N.Y.C. You encouraged and inspired me to never give up and you truly believed in me. Anne Frelich, Jackie Lastique and Millie Colon.

In the Family of Women there are so many women to acknowledge that I would need several pages. Clair Foster who was my buddy for one cycle and challenged me to pick a big goal that was important to me, that I started but never completed. Clair your support meant the world to me. Thank you.

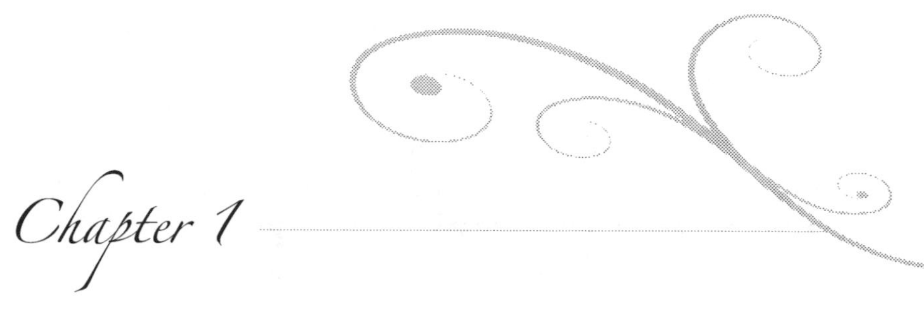

Chapter 1

While many children are fortunate enough to have a peaceful, loving childhood with a comfortable home and nurturing, loving parents who care and provide for them, such was not the case with me. Yet, somehow, I managed to not only survive but also thrive as I grew up. As you read my story, I hope it will uplift and inspire you.

I was born on a cold and snowy day in 1950 at St. Catherine's Hospital in Brooklyn, New York. My mother brought me home to 666 Broadway in Brooklyn. We lived there for the first three years of my life.

I lived with my mother, father, and two older sisters. June was four when I was born, and Annie was three. From photos of myself as a child, I see that I was cute, with light brownish, curly hair and chubby red cheeks.

My mother, Frances Graziano Goldberg, was heavyset, with brown hair and brown eyes. If you'd met her back then, she would have been smoking a cigarette. It was her trademark. One was always hanging out of her mouth.

My father, Morton Goldberg, was almost bald, but what little hair he had was brown. He had blue eyes, missing teeth, and a ruddy complexion. He was only a few inches taller than my mother. And, like my mother, he smoked. In fact, I don't remember him ever being without a cigarette.

My mother was thirty-eight when my parents married on October 29, 1940. My sister June was born in 1946, and Annie in 1947. I came along after they had been married for ten years.

The five of us lived in a tiny, four-room apartment on the second floor of a three-story tenement. I was told the hallway was dark, and the apartment was crowded, cluttered, and dirty. Ashtrays were everywhere, and often a lit cigarette rested on one of them. Dirty dishes piled up in the kitchen sink alongside an old wooden table and four chairs. There was also an old highchair for me. One of our bedrooms had bunk beds in one corner and my crib in the other. In the living room, there was a brown plaid cloth couch with a ripped plastic cover over it. In front of the couch was the television. The back room of the apartment was my parents' bedroom. The apartment had one window in each room. The windows had shades with brown plaid curtains. During the day, Mother often had the shades up since the apartment was not well lit.

I cried a lot as a young child. When I needed a diaper change, I cried. When I was hungry, I cried. My mother took her sweet time to see what I needed. Sometimes I gave myself a headache from crying so much. At least one time, I remember my mother yelling, "If you don't stop crying, I will give you something to cry about!"

I usually just cried more until I fell asleep. I longed to be held, but that didn't happen often.

My two older sisters were not much older than I was, and they also had needs. Once in a while, though, one of them took me out of the playpen and played with me. I loved it when they gave me attention.

I don't believe my mother spent much time with me because I was either with my sisters or my cousins who lived downstairs. Mother was overwhelmed with all of us. My father wasn't around much. The fights with my mother and the tension in the apartment kept him away.

I hated when their voices began to rise. I knew there was going to be a screaming match. It made me tremble and sweat with fear.

My father had been discharged from the army in 1944 and was only working a part-time job by the time I came along. He left the apartment early in the morning, and when he finally came home, he was usually drunk. He would start complaining about something. "Frances, I am gone all day, and you are still in front of the television. What are we having for dinner?"

Mother's response was "Order something out, if you have any money left and didn't spend it all on liquor. I am not cooking today. I have a headache, and my back hurts."

We would eat eventually. But not until my mother was good and ready and her television program was over.

There was always something to fight about with the two of them. My father yelled for my mother to clean the house, do the dishes, cook for us, and change our clothes. It was all on my mother. My father felt that it wasn't his job, yet he was working only part-time and spent most of his money in the bar.

Both my parents were alcoholics and addicted to cigarettes. The apartment smelled of cigarette smoke. The rare times my mother put me on her lap, I choked from the smoke.

With very little money and five mouths to feed, my mother was always depressed, overwhelmed, and angry at the world. She yelled and lashed out verbally. Her face was always tense. I never saw her smile. She had a lot to escape from, and alcohol, cigarettes, and television were her escape.

Uncle Sydney's Visits

One bright spot in my life at that time was Uncle Sydney, my father's younger brother. He looked a lot like my father. He was also bald on top, and the little hair he had was brown.

Uncle Sydney worked as the neighborhood bookie, hanging out at the pub and the clubs, where he drank and smoked. Gamblers placed bets with him. If they won, he paid out. If not, he kept the money. When he made money, he helped my mother and father.

I loved Uncle Sydney. When he was around, he was kind. He picked me up in the air and gave me a big hug. It brought joy to my little heart. I giggled and enjoyed his attention. He bought me pretty dresses when he had money. Once he said, "Ruthie, let your mother dress you in your favorite blue dress, and I will take you outside for a walk."

Mother heard him but pretended she didn't. Her television show was more important.

My sister June (who was only six) said, "I will dress Ruthie." And she did. She washed me, changed my diaper, kissed me, and tickled me. She loved it when I smiled and giggled.

Going outside with Uncle Sydney meant I was going to have ice cream, and that gave me goose bumps just thinking about it. These rare occasions when Uncle Sydney came during the day were my favorite times. He usually came late at night after work when I was asleep.

Aunt Jessie lived downstairs with her husband, Uncle Hyme (my father's older brother), and my three cousins. When I was born, Warren was four, Robert was three, and Arthur was around eight months.

I loved being around my cousins. They were always nice to me. Until they had their own television, they asked permission to come up to our apartment to watch television with us. Aunt Jessie often came up with them. Sometimes she walked into the apartment and started complaining to my mother. "Frances, your kids are dirty. Change their clothes."

Mother ignored her.

"When do you intend to wash the dishes in the sink?" my aunt asked.

My mother replied, "If it bothers you, go downstairs."

Aunt Jessie left.

Later in life, Aunt Jessie reminded me, "Your mother was lazy and never took care of you children properly. Your clothes were always dirty, and the apartment was always cluttered and a mess."

Honestly, I hated listening to Aunt Jessie tell these stories. I wanted to protect my mother, but I knew there was no defense I could give. When my mother had to meet with the welfare office or keep other appointments, she left me with Aunt Jessie. Usually, Aunt Jessie complained. "Why didn't your mother wash and change you before leaving you with me?"

I guess Aunt Jessie needed to complain since she couldn't change my mother. Then she gave me a sponge bath. I felt cared for. I loved the attention. She put a fresh diaper on me and dressed me. Then she fed me lunch or dinner. It was either chicken soup, an egg sandwich, or something similar. Often in the afternoon, she put me down for a nap after taking care of me. I loved feeling clean and fresh. I usually fell right to sleep, safe and secure. Sometimes Aunt Jessie sounded stern, but she wasn't. It was just her way.

Aunt Jessie was a wonderful aunt. Her apartment was spotless. You could eat off the floors. She had four rooms. It was also a small apartment, but it was night and day from my apartment upstairs. It was well lit, with pretty, bright colors of yellow, light green, and other cheerful colors. The kitchen was a nice size, and everything was spotless. When I stayed over, the couch in the living room opened up into a daybed. Aunt Jessie and Uncle Hyme had the back room. It was large enough to have little Arthur's crib in there with them. The two older boys had the smaller room off the living room, and it was perfect for them.

When Aunt Jessie wasn't available to watch me, Mother took me with her to the neighborhood bar. The bar smelled strongly of beer. The bar had big, wooden, round stools with wooden backs. The floors were filled with sawdust. Most of the people had cigarettes hanging out of their mouths or in the ashtrays. For some reason, they just let a cigarette burn in the ashtray until it went out. I hated the smell of liquor and the fog of smoke. There were jumbo peanuts on the bar and peanut shells everywhere.

I hated being in the bar, especially when everyone was drunk. Some of the men liked to pat me on the head and tell my mother how cute I was as I sat on a barstool next to her.

One day, my mother knocked on Aunt Jessie's door and said,

"Jessie, could you take care of Ruthie for a week? I have several appointments for June and Annie."

Aunt Jessie said, "Okay, Frances, but make sure you come back for her."

By this time, my cousins had their own television. It was fun watching cartoons with them. After a week, Aunt Jessie had not heard from my mother. Another week passed, and she still hadn't heard from her.

"Where is your mother?" Aunt Jessie wondered aloud. "Did she just abandon you? She better get back here soon."

Finally, Mother returned.

Aunt Jessie was furious with her and yelled, "Why didn't you call me and ask for more time?"

Mother said, "I am sorry. I had no way of phoning you. But can Ruthie stay with you for a little while longer? I promise I will come for her soon."

Aunt Jessie, being a caring woman, and also because she knew what was really going on, said, "Okay, but make it fast. You better get your daughter out of here. I cannot take care of her much longer."

I ran into the bedroom, crying my eyes out. All I could think was, *Nobody wants me. Nobody cares about me. I don't belong to anybody. Nobody loves me.*

I stayed with Aunt Jessie a little more than three weeks. I didn't care about not being with my mother because I loved being with Aunt Jessie, Uncle Hyme, and my three cousins.

Finally, however, my mother returned. She took me to All Saints Roman Catholic Church to be baptized, although I was three years old and children were usually baptized when they were infants. I had no idea where my sisters were or why my mother had suddenly decided I needed to be baptized, but I was about to find out.

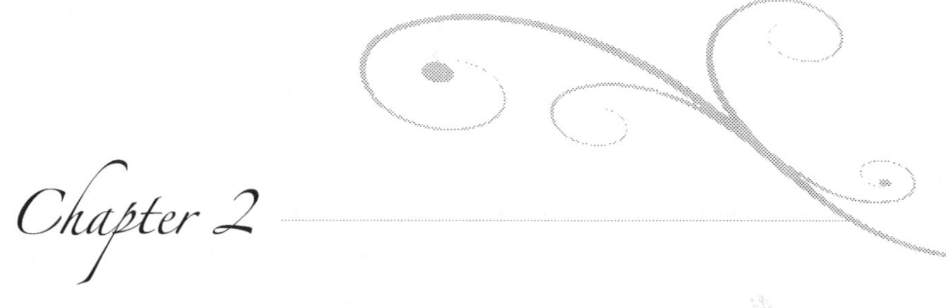

Chapter 2

On April 8, 1953, a sunny spring day, Mother and I got into a big yellow cab. She didn't say a word.

"Mom, where are we going?" I asked.

"Sit back and be quiet. We will be there soon," she answered.

My stomach churned. I was about to throw up.

We stopped in front of a massive building, and I thought, *What is this building and why have we stopped?* My head started to pound. I trembled.

St. Joseph's Hall Orphanage

As it turned out, Mother had brought me to St. Joseph's Hall Orphanage for girls. When I look back on that day, I am grateful that she chose to bring me to a safe home where I could be taken care of by the Sisters of Charity of New York. Their mission is to dedicate their lives to the service of the poor for the glory of God. Given my first few years of life, I can see now that I was blessed to have had this opportunity. I learned to know and love God throughout my life, and in the hardest times, I turned to faith for courage and perseverance.

The building and grounds of St. Joseph's took up several city blocks. The orphanage had five floors and an attic, and the entire building was surrounded by an iron fence. In one section by the playground area, there were massive amounts of barbed wire for safety purposes. On the top of the building hung a cross.

St. Joseph's Hall Orphanage held eighty or more girls at a time. It was located at 735 Willoughby Avenue, Brooklyn, New York, in the Bedford Stuyvesant section. The Sisters of Charity of New York were the main caretakers. Laywomen also worked with the girls. The girls were children whose parents came under hard times and could not afford to take care of them.

My mother made this gut-wrenching decision to place me in the orphanage. She did not have a job, my father had left her, and she needed time to get her life together. I didn't know it, but my two sisters, Annie and June, had been placed in the orphanage one month earlier.

Annie, Ruthie, and June, Mom in background

Mother held my hand as we got out of the taxi, and we walked up giant steps to a huge, wooden door. She rang the bell. As we waited, I became tearful and felt panicky.

A woman with a beautiful black dress, a cape wrapped around her shoulders, and a bonnet on her head with a big bow under her chin came to the door. What a big smile! "Welcome," she said.

As we entered the lobby, on one wall, above a big, shiny brown table, was a large picture of a woman dressed the same as the lady who had opened the door. I later found out the woman in the picture was Saint Elizabeth Ann Seton. Mother Seton was the foundress of the Sisters of Charity of New York.

In the huge lobby, we waited in big brown leather chairs as the lady went into the office. I noticed the shiny floors as I sat shaking and wondering, *What am I doing here?*

Tears streamed down my face as a beautiful lady dressed in white appeared. Except for the color, her clothing was identical to the lady who had welcomed us. This woman smiled and escorted us into the office. She said, "I am Sister Anne Marie. What is your name?"

I said, "My name is Ruthie."

Sister asked me several more questions, and I began to feel calmer. The only way I can describe Sister Anne Marie is angelical, kind, and caring. She then introduced me to Sister Joseph, who had the same black habit as the sister who answered the door. Sister Joseph let me know that she would be taking care of me and would be back shortly.

Meanwhile, another sister took my mother to the back area of the office to handle paperwork. After the paperwork was completed, Sister brought me back to the lobby. She held me and continued to ask me questions to distract me. Meanwhile, Mother left the building without saying goodbye.

When I realized what had happened, I became hysterical, screaming, "Mommy! Mommy!" and I sobbed. I couldn't stop. I thought, *Why didn't she take me with her?* Fear and despair took possession of me completely.

At this point, Sister took me in her arms and walked me back into the office. She held me, saying, "It will be okay."

When I stopped sobbing, Sister Joseph returned to take me to lunch. She said, "Ruthie, are you hungry?"

I said, "Yes."

Sister Joseph took my hand and told me I was going to meet

other little girls like me. She escorted me down a massive staircase to the basement floor. We entered a huge room where many other girls were sitting at tables waiting for lunch.

Sister announced, "Miss Ruth, I would like to introduce Ruthie. She is new and is ready for lunch." Sister handed me over to Ms. Ruth.

Ms. Ruth was one of the counselors for my age group.

Sister Joseph said, "Ruthie, I will see you later during naptime," and she left.

The dining room was big, with many girls sitting around the tables talking, laughing, and making a lot of noise. I was escorted to an empty seat, and Ms. Ruth introduced me to the other girls. She said, "Ruthie is new to St. Joseph's. She just arrived. Who would like to help her with lunch?"

I stood there paralyzed with fear of the unknown.

Several of the girls raised their hands, and Ms. Ruth called on a girl named Lucy, who had a big smile.

Each girl at the table of five also smiled and then introduced herself. It helped me feel more relaxed. The girls were nice.

When lunch was ready, Sister Michael came from the kitchen and asked us to settle down. She said, "The lunch is ready. Let us pray."

The girls knew that meant no more talking. The room was completely silent.

Sister started us with "Bless us, oh Lord, and these thy gifts, which we are about to receive, from thy bounty, through Christ our Lord. Amen."

After prayer, the food wagon came out, and lunch was served. The counselors took the food to each table.

After lunch, my group was taken to the playground. Ms. Ruth kept her eye on me as I stood by myself, feeling alone, scared, and frightened. I missed my mother so much and kept wondering when she was going to come and get me. Other girls approached me, but I was too shy and scared to talk to them. After an hour, we were taken to our dormitory for our afternoon nap.

Sister Joseph was in the dormitory when we arrived. When she saw me, she approached saying, "Ruthie, I will show you around, and then we will come into my room to complete some paperwork."

The dormitory was massive, with at least six rows of beds. Next to each bed was a nightstand. The bathroom was long in length and had at least five stalls and five sinks.

Sister showed me where I would be sleeping. She then took me into her private room and tried to comfort me. She saw how terrified I was. She asked me several questions and completed her intake form. She was loving and caring, and I felt her kindness. When we got back to the main room of the dormitory, all the other girls were napping. Sister brought me to her rocking chair in the middle of the room, placed me on her lap, and rocked me to sleep.

I woke up frightened and startled; I had forgotten where I was. I cried. But Sister held me and said, "Ruthie, don't be afraid. You will be all right. I will take care of you."

After several days of being in the orphanage, I was told that my pierced earrings had to be removed. The very idea of removing the gold loop earrings that my mother had given me gave me a crushing sensation in my body. Sister Teresa, the nurse, brought me into the infirmary and took out my earrings. She tried to explain that they wanted to prevent infection, but it was difficult to understand her reasoning. That night, I cried myself to sleep. I had lost my only connection to my mother, and I was devastated.

Connecting with My Sisters

After naptime, we were usually taken to the playground again. This particular day, many girls were playing. Several counselors watched over us. School was out for the day, and the older girls were also outside. Some of the older girls were friendly. Girls were enjoying the merry-go-round, and it seemed like fun. One of the girls asked if I wanted to try it. She helped me up and showed me how to sit and hold on to the railings. I loved being on the merry-go-round. It was exciting as the wind blew in my face. One of the girls took charge of spinning us around. It was one of my favorite rides. I loved being with the older girls. I didn't feel so shy.

After I had enough of spinning around, I walked over to the swings. As I stood there, I thought, *How much fun it would be to try the swings.* A girl said, "Would you like a ride on the swing?" She saw I was standing there, but I was too scared to try it on my own. The girl looked familiar, but I didn't recognize her right away because I just didn't expect my sister Annie to be there.

At first, Annie didn't recognize me either. Before she lifted me up onto the swing, she said, "What is your name?"

"Ruthie Goldberg," I said.

Annie smiled. "My name is Annie Goldberg. We're sisters."

We were elated to have found each other. We hugged as tears of joy streamed down our faces. Annie put me on the swing, and it was so much fun. Knowing Annie was there eased my mind a little.

After I got off the swing, Annie said, "Did you see June yet?"

"No," I said, but anticipation filled my heart.

"Let's find her," said Annie. "She would love to see you."

Annie escorted me to Ms. Ruth and said, "She is June Goldberg's sister. Can we find June, so they can see each other?"

We located June. I ran into her arms. She hugged me, and I felt happy, loved, and safe being with my two sisters.

Because of our age differences, Annie and June were in different groups. Whenever I had a chance to see them or spend time with them, I did. Spending time with them gave me a sense of belonging. At this time in my life, my sisters meant everything to me; we were family. Whenever we were in the playground and I saw June, I'd run over to her to give her a hug. It brought so much joy to my heart. I saw Annie a little more often, and once in a while, she let me play with her and her friends. I felt happy just to see my sisters. I didn't see them daily, sometimes not for weeks. Yet I knew they were in the building, and that made me happy.

The big room in the orphanage was usually used for activities, parties, visits with family, or when the girls in various groups were brought together for a few hours. On the rare occasion when our groups were all together, or when the weather was extreme, either raining or snowing, and I got the opportunity to be with my sisters, I loved it. I looked forward to those times. The three of us played a game together, and my sister June was bossy, but I didn't mind. After all, she was my big sister.

I loved being around June. When it was only my group in the playroom, once in a while, I asked permission to leave and visit June for a few minutes. I usually kept my word and came back when required. When June saw me in her division, as I walked toward her section of the room where she had a bed, a dresser, and a chair, she yelled, "Don't touch my stuff!" in a loving way that only June could say. I loved looking at her personal things, and she didn't like it, but sometimes she let me. When we saw each other, we hugged, and I felt so good afterward. We were family.

On the other hand, whenever the opportunity arose, I looked in Annie's locker, and often, if I saw something I liked, her response was "Keep it. It's yours." I still love that about her. She has always been kind and generous.

Usually on Saturday evening, we all received an allowance. I think it was twenty-five cents. The candy store opened up, and we were allowed to spend our quarter on candy. My favorite candy was a Sugar Daddy pop. I loved the caramel flavor, and it lasted a long time. When we all had bought our candy, we went into the big room and watched a movie. This was a fun night. Some movies I remembered were *Dumbo*, *Peter Pan*, *Alice in Wonderland*, and *Pinocchio*. I am sure there were many more. My favorite was *Pinocchio* because it had a moral to it—don't tell a lie. Before the movie began, we had some free time while girls were buying their candy and getting settled. Once in a while, I used some of my allowance to buy Sister Bridget a soda. I ran to her division and gave it to her before the movie began. I did it with one purpose in mind, so she would be a little nicer to my sister Annie.

Sister Bridget was Annie's caretaker. Annie didn't like her. She felt Sister didn't like her either, because she picked on her often. Maybe Annie was a discipline problem, but I didn't see it that way, and neither did Annie. Once in a while, we were together with the girls in Annie's division because the television set was in their dormitory. At that time, my division's sleeping quarters were right next door. But the lavatory was also in Annie's dormitory, so often I would pretend to need to go to the bathroom just so I could run over to Annie's bed and kiss her hello. I loved it when I had this opportunity. During this particular time, I saw my sister Annie a little more often. We sometimes sat next to each other while watching television. One night, Sister Bridget said, "Annie Goldberg, what are you doing up? Get to bed."

I was so hurt. It wasn't the only time I heard her yelling at my sister.

Visiting Day

Visiting day at St. Joseph's was Sunday after church and breakfast. Our parents would show up and take us into the huge room for a visit. Each week, many of us waited by the door where the visitors entered. I can't recall how often I waited for my mother to show up, but she rarely did. As I waited a half hour and realized she was not coming, I walked away as tears streamed down my face. Week after week, I felt sadness. Little did I know that my mother had started another family and was busy with her new children, Maryann and Connie, and the new man she lived with, Jimmy.

Often, my father came to visit. I loved those times. I was happy that he cared. He always came with candy. Usually, he had several snacks: popcorn, potato chips, cheese doodles, pretzels, peanuts. I loved that most of all. My heart almost burst out of my chest when Dad first wanted to put me on his lap. He was a stranger, and I didn't feel comfortable. I slowly began to trust him. My father's visit became the highlight of my week. Once in a while, Dad brought Uncle Sydney with him. I loved seeing him. Knowing they tried their best to see me brought me closer to them. One time, my father came to visit me on crutches. I knew then how much he loved me. But I also knew he could not be the one to take me out of the orphanage. The question in my mind was, *Will I ever get to go home?*

Annie, June, Ruthie, and Daddy in background

Chapter 3

My years in the orphanage shaped my life, in both positive and negative ways. Yet I grew up as a positive child. It became clear to me early on that life's not always fair, or sweet like peaches and cream, but I can choose to see things any way I want. It is up to me to learn from my mistakes and to find forgiveness in my heart for any disappointments I encounter along the way. I had some big disappointments and upsets, and I made many mistakes during my formative years.

At the orphanage, we spent a lot of our free time at the playground. That was where we could let off energy from the day, which helped, especially during the years I attended school.

I loved my free time and always wanted to play and have fun. One day, I wanted to play dodgeball with some of the girls. I thought I would be good at it. I was excited to be on the team. I waited with anticipation. The leaders of the game began picking sides. As I waited to be picked for one of the teams, I felt butterflies in my stomach. I waited each time for my name to be called, but it did not happen until the very end. I didn't understand why I was the last girl picked for the team. I trembled with fear. I had to prove to the girls that I belonged on the team. I tried hard to play well, but I was out on the first try. I ran to the corner of the playground and cried. I was embarrassed, disappointed, and sorry I didn't get to prove myself.

My inability to play well and my expectations of believing I could be good instead proved to me that I wasn't good enough. Being the last girl picked for one of the teams also reinforced my feelings of not being liked by other girls, and it hurt. That night, I told Sister Joseph how I felt.

"Ruthie, it is only a game," she said. "Picking you last had nothing to do with not liking you but with your skill at dodgeball. If you still want to play, you will get better."

I didn't want to play again.

When I look back now, I realize Sister was right. I was new to the game, they didn't know me, and they didn't want to take a chance on me. It had nothing to do with my worth as a person.

One lesson I learned in life is there will be disappointments, but I can pick myself up and move on. I can choose to not take anything personally but instead use it as an opportunity to grow.

Being Bullied

Once a girl in the playground decided to tease me. At the time, I didn't understand why she needed to bully me. But later on, I realized it was because my last name was Goldberg, and we were in a Catholic orphanage. She was a big girl and scary looking. I have to admit I was afraid of her. She chased me around the playground, calling me "Jew ball." I hated when she did that. It was cruel and unkind to make fun of me because I am half-Jewish. It frightened me and made me anxious, and my heart sank as I ran fast enough so she wouldn't catch me. I never knew what would happen if she did catch me because I always ran next to a counselor. This happened several times before I got up the nerve to tell Sister. Sister told her to stop teasing me or she would be punished. She finally did stop. This was the first time I realized being half-Jewish was not acceptable to some people.

Another Difficult Experience at the Playground

We spent time at the playground when the skies were blue and the sun was brightly shining, when it was freezing cold, and even sometimes when snow was on the ground. As I mentioned before, the only time we did not go to the playground was when it was raining or snowing heavily. The playground was an important part of our social interaction and our physical activities for good health. There were always several counselors watching over us. A counselor waited at the door for security reasons and in case a girl had to use the bathroom. Usually, we had to stay outside until the bell rang, and then we knew it was time to go back inside. But one time, I was so cold I felt as though my feet and hands were frostbitten. I went to the counselor and said, "Miss Teresa, I am so cold I can hardly stand it. Can I go inside?"

Miss Teresa shook her head and said, "Ruthie, you know the rules. You must wait until the bell rings."

I couldn't believe she had no compassion for me. I was hurt and felt rejected. I thought, *Doesn't she understand I can't stand the cold any longer*? But I knew it was useless to argue or try to convince her. I found a cardboard box in the yard that was underneath an open shed and put myself inside it to stay warm. I brought my knees up to my chin and my hands in between my thighs as I sat there shivering. I felt sorry for myself and wondered if the bell would ever ring as I waited and waited. When it was time to go back inside, I ran to the door.

When I look back on this experience, I realize that if every girl wanted to go inside because they were cold, it would have been chaos. Miss Teresa probably felt we were young enough to withstand the cold.

Nightmares

After dinner, we usually went up to our dormitories for the evening, unless some other event was taking place. Our dormitory had a huge open space. The tables and chairs were on one side of the room, and the rows of beds in the middle and on the other side. There was often time for us to be at the tables and play board games or color pictures. Sometimes, Sister would read us a story of the life of a saint. I loved those times. Also, on the rare occasion, we got to watch a television show. The television was brought in on wheels, and when the show was over, it was wheeled out.

When it was time to prepare for bed, we lined up outside the bathrooms and took turns getting washed up. Then we went to our bed and put on our pajamas. When we were all settled, Sister announced, "It is time for night prayer." That meant silence. After night prayer, we were expected to go to sleep.

Sometimes at night, I felt afraid to go to sleep. My bed was facing a window with a fire escape, and when I looked up, I saw someone outside the window staring at me. My heart pounded. It took me a long time to calm down and fall asleep. I stuck my head under the pillow and eventually fell asleep. I didn't realize there couldn't possibly be anyone on the fire escape. As soon as it was light outside, the person was gone. Eventually, Sister moved my bed to another section of the room, and I was so relieved.

During the night, if we had to go to the bathroom, Sister expected us to just go. Many times, I had a recurring dream that prevented me from going. I dreamt that I went into the bathroom, and in the stall next to me, there was a witch sitting on the seat. She was laughing and hissing. I was terrified to go to the bathroom by myself at night. Sometimes, I actually wet the bed. I was embarrassed to tell anyone and afraid of getting in trouble. I made my bed with the wet sheet in hopes that it would dry on its own. It usually left a big yellow stain, but only I saw it at night. We changed our underwear every morning, so I was able to hide my underpants. I just waited until sheet-exchange day. As far as I know, no one ever found out.

Another Painful Experience

I was five and a half years old when Sister Joseph was transferred from our age group. It broke my heart that I was not going to see her every day. I was attached to her, especially since she had taken care of me since I was three. I knew she loved me, and I loved her.

Sister Joseph became responsible for all the divisions. She actually lived in my sister June's division. Once in a while, I saw Sister Joseph. When I saw her, I ran up to her and gave her a hug. It made me happy.

Sister Henry became my new caretaker. She liked me and always gave me a hug. I loved being around her, and I received plenty of positive attention. One particular day was an exception and one of the most painful experiences of my orphanage years. I was in line waiting to use the bathroom and to wash up before bed. Sister must have been in a bad mood because usually she let us talk in line. This time was different. There was a lot of chatter from the girls. It upset Sister. She said, "I want you to stand in line in silence so we can move this along more quickly."

The girls continued to talk, and Sister banged a stick on the floor, and it made a loud noise.

"No more talking," said Sister. "The next girl who talks will be punished severely."

I had been quiet the entire time, but just as Sister said no more talking for the second time, the girl behind me said something mean to me, and I told her to leave me alone. Sister saw me talk and yelled, "Ruthie, get out of the line and come over here."

I was shaken up because I really wasn't talking. I tried to explain, but Sister wouldn't listen.

"Your mouth was moving," she said. Then she turned to the

other girls. "I will show you all what happens when you disrespect me and don't listen." She smacked me hard.

My heart raced. I couldn't breathe. I was shaking and crying. There was not one sound in the line or in the bathroom. You could have heard a pin drop.

Sister dragged me to the middle of the room while everyone was settling in bed. She said, "If you don't stop crying, Ruthie, I will give you something to cry about."

I cried harder, and she hit me again. I couldn't believe Sister Henry, of all sisters, would be so mean. I thought she loved me and cared about me, but she wasn't treating me like she did.

Finally, Sister told me to get into bed.

I did, but I continued to cry. I couldn't stop. I was so hurt that she didn't care about me. It wasn't my fault that I talked. I was defending myself. I felt so rejected and mistreated.

It felt like I cried for hours, but it was probably more like fifteen minutes. Sister finally came over to see if I was okay. She told me to calm down, and she gave me two pills and some water.

The next day, Sister acted as if the experience had never happened. Later, I knew she was sorry because she singled me out to help her. She often sent me on errands and let me stay up later than the other girls.

Once I was asked if I wanted to help Sister Henry with Christmas. It meant I got to stay up late. I had no idea what she had in mind, but I said yes. I loved helping her. I felt she cared again. This particular day, I found out that Santa Claus was not real. It was a big disappointment. As Sister wrapped the gifts and put the name on the sticky, I placed the sticky on the package and put the gift under the tree. I did this feeling sadness and disappointment as I realized there was no Santa Claus. I didn't say anything to Sister. If I did, she would have helped me to understand.

Another Painful Experience

I got blamed for hiding food I did not want to eat behind the refrigerator. It hurt badly to be blamed for something I did not do. After the above experience, if I was accused or blamed for something I did not do, I overreacted. This experience affected me for a long time.

During mealtime, we went to our assigned seats. Every few months, we got different seats so we could get to know other girls. One time, my assigned seat was very close to the refrigerator in the enormous dining room. Often, I saw girls lean down by the corner of the refrigerator. Our table was small and so close to the refrigerator that for a while I never thought anything of it.

One day, I got curious to see why girls bent down to the corner of the refrigerator. So, when no one was looking, I bent down to look, and to my surprise, it was horrible and shocking! I felt nauseated. It smelled bad. All sorts of foods were mashed into the back of the refrigerator. Some of it had turned brown, mushy and rotten. Other foods were fresh, so it had recently been put there—carrots, beans, corn, rhubarb pie, and lots of other stuff I couldn't make out. I just knew it was awful. I ran over to Sister Henry and told her what I saw. I usually am not a tattletale, but this was so gross I had to tell somebody. I didn't give Sister any names. I didn't want to get anyone in trouble. But when she pulled the refrigerator out, her face turned red, and she slammed things around. "Whoever did this will be punished," she said.

I felt so bad that I offered to help clean up the mess.

At this time, I was living in a different dormitory space. The main room was large, with twelve beds in it and a big, empty space in the middle where we gathered for short meetings. It also had Sister's private bedroom built inside this huge room. There were also two bedrooms next door to the main bedroom, with a small hallway in between. In each of the small bedrooms, there were six beds. These bedrooms were for girls who, according to Sister, were responsible and did not wet the bed. There were around twenty of us in this age group.

After dinner, we went up to our rooms. This one night, when Sister arrived, it was obvious she wasn't happy. She went to the loudspeaker and in a perturbed voice said, "Every girl needs to be in her pajamas and in the main room in ten minutes, and I do not want to hear a sound."

All the girls gathered in the main room as instructed and wondered why Sister was upset. They all piled in and took a seat on the floor in complete silence.

Sister began lecturing us. "How terrible it is to find food behind the refrigerator," she said. "You should be grateful to have food to eat. There are so many starving children in the world who would love to have the food you wasted. It is a sin to waste food. Those who put food behind the refrigerator were ungrateful, and if they do not confess to doing it, this whole group will not be allowed to take part in any of the Christmas activities."

Christmas was in a few weeks, and we all loved Christmas. There were many parties, and people came in to entertain us and bring gifts. It was always so much fun. On Christmas morning, after breakfast, we were taken into the living room, and a large, beautiful tree was all decorated with many gifts under it. Sister called each one of us to give us a gift with our name on it. In the late morning, our families visited us or took us out for the day. None of us wanted to miss out on any of this. I thought, *I wish I had never looked behind the refrigerator and reported it to Sister. She is furious, and this is a serious matter.*

Sister was sitting there frowning, raising her eyebrows, and pouting. She said the girls had to admit their faults or we would all be punished.

I wondered who would confess to this awful thing. As we sat there, it seemed like forever. Then Sister said, "If you have ever put food behind the refrigerator, please stand up. We will stay here all night if girls don't tell the truth."

We all sat there for another fifteen minutes. Finally, one girl stood up and said, "Sister, I put food I didn't like behind the refrigerator."

Another girl stood up and admitted it, then another, and before I knew it, there were at least six girls standing. I was happy that we would not miss out on Christmas and that we could go to bed soon. But instead of letting us go to bed, Sister said, "There is one girl who did not stand up and confess. If she doesn't, she will be severely punished for not owning up to her disgraceful actions."

I looked around the room, wondering, *Who could it be?*

We sat, waiting for this girl to stand up. It felt like a long time, and then Sister said, "Okay. Everyone can go to bed without talking. I don't want to hear a sound out of any of you. But, Ruth Goldberg, you stay here."

I was shocked that she was asking me to stay.

Then Sister said, "You will stand out in the hall until you confess to your actions."

I was devastated. I hadn't done anything wrong.

I stood in the hall sobbing, wondering why she was picking on me. I just couldn't understand why she thought I was guilty. I stood in the hall for several hours, upset and confused. My stomach hurt, and my head pounded. Then I had to go to the bathroom—bad! I had to do something. I thought about running to the sister's bathroom around the corner, close by our rooms, but I knew if Sister saw me, or if another sister was in the bathroom, I would be in big trouble. Our bathroom was in the older girls' dormitory, and I knew I couldn't use that bathroom without permission. After a while, I realized I needed to tell a lie and confess that I was guilty, or else I would end up wetting my pajamas. I knocked on Sister Henry's door.

Sister came out and said, "Are you ready to confess?"

"Yes, Sister, I did it," I said. "Can I go to the bathroom now please?" I raced to the bathroom.

When I returned, Sister was waiting for me. "Now go to bed," she said. "Tomorrow we will discuss this further. You will be punished from several of the Christmas celebrations since you did not confess when the other girls did."

Chapter 4

While I was in the orphanage, I loved going to Shoreham, Long Island, New York, for summer camp. Each age group got to spend a month at camp, away from the city. I cannot remember one time that I didn't love being at camp. It filled my heart with so much joy and excitement.

When summer began, I knew going to camp was around the corner. Camp was my favorite place to be. When it was our time to go to camp each year, Sister asked, "Who would like to volunteer to go up into the storage room to help bring down the suitcases?"

"I do," I said.

My hand was always the first one up. When I was three, four, or five, Sister said, "Ruthie, when you grow up, you can volunteer." She smiled and patted me on the head.

Finally, I was old enough to volunteer. I liked going up the huge, wooden staircase. I also enjoyed looking at all the stuff. Our suitcases were on the right, and on the left were old altars that were no longer useable, old religious statues that were in some way broken, and some that were just old. As I climbed up the steps, I saw an old altar with a baby Jesus statue sitting on top. I looked at the statue (it's hard to describe the experience, even today, because words fall short) and felt so much love. I couldn't help staring at baby Jesus. At that moment, I intuitively knew that I was a child of God. I felt love moving through my body. When I look back on the experience, I realize it was my first encounter with God. I looked forward to climbing those steps every year. But only once did I have that extraordinary experience.

Soon, we were taken out of the city and brought to St. Joseph's summer camp. I loved being in the country with the fresh air, the woods, and the beach. I loved the ocean and the sand. When the day came to leave for camp, we were all enthusiastic. During the ride, we sang songs almost all the way to the site. I loved listening to other girls sing. When we arrived at the camp entrance, we all anticipated getting off the bus. We cheered and clapped. Sister announced, "We need to make sure we do not leave anything on the bus. As we get off the bus, line up in assigned pairs, and I want complete silence until we arrive at the Big House."

The Big House was up the hill, and we had to suppress our excitement for a few minutes until we arrived at the front door. There were several sisters waiting to greet us. Once we were in the house, we all began chattering. Then our names were called, and we were divided into groups.

On one side of the Big House (which was what we called the main building) were the sleeping quarters, which had several rows of beds. The other side of the room consisted of a full-size dining room, a big kitchen, the laundry room, the infirmary, the chapel, and private bedroom suites for the sisters. Outside the main building was beautiful landscaping. The grass was perfectly manicured. There were bushes, and flowers, and lots of greenery, and our own private beach.

Taking walks through the woods and going to the beach to play were activities I looked forward to. When I woke up in the morning, the first thing I did was look outside. When the sun was out, I smiled. I knew it was going to be another great day.

At the beach, I loved playing in the sand with my pail and shovel. Either I played with other girls or by myself, building sandcastles or big holes to pour water into. Sometimes, when we had permission, I went off by myself collecting shells or rocks. We had some freedom since we couldn't go too far in either direction. St. Joseph's camp was private, and the beach area in both directions for quite a distance was also private.

Little Ruthie at the beach with Sister and other girls in background

At a certain age, when we were at the beach and wanted to go to the bathroom, we were given permission to go up to the Big House by ourselves. One time, instead of walking up the steps, I decided to be adventurous, and I walked in the sand, up to the top of the short hill, without my sneakers. For fun, I made up these little games for myself. This time, I stepped on a rusty nail. As it went deep into my foot, I thought, *I am in trouble!* My foot hurt so bad I limped the rest of the way and went into the main house crying my eyes out. One of the sisters saw me and brought me into the infirmary. I thought I would get yelled at for being where I did not belong, but instead Sister was kind, caring, and concerned. She cleaned my wound, took out the nail, and put a bandage on my foot. She told me I had to get a tetanus shot.

I was frightened with jitters in my stomach. I closed my eyes tight, and before I knew it, it was over. Sister gave me a cookie and a lollypop. I felt safe and cared for. Sister informed me that I had to wait in the infirmary until the girls came up from the beach. I didn't mind since my foot wasn't hurting as much, and Sister was kind to me.

When we went into the woods, we walked alongside the road and passed blackberry bushes, flowers, and even some birds and snakes. A favorite game I liked was called *a treasure hunt.* The game was set up by the counselors before we took our walk. The counselor told us the rules and explained that the clues were attached to the trees. We had to find the tree that had the clues and then "find the treasure." It was so much fun, and even more fun the few times I found the treasure.

Another activity I enjoyed was going to the arts and crafts cottage. I saw the sign in big letters on the front door—*Arts and Crafts.* I loved every chance I had to be there. As we approached the cottage, my excitement bubbled up. We always had fun making unique items. We got to pick out the activity we wanted to do out of three choices. Therefore, if we didn't finish something from the previous time, we could work on it again. I remember making a pair of earrings with sequins. I also remember making a potholder. We made fans with ice-cream sticks and colored them with bright colors. We cut out shapes and designs on colored paper. I used paints and colored pens to color in the drawings or designs.

I felt disappointment when we had to clean up, as it was almost time to end. I never wanted to leave the arts and crafts room. It brought so much joy.

After dinner, at least four nights a week, unless it was raining, we had a campfire. We gathered around the fire in a circle, and I loved being close to the front. This was another one of my favorite activities. Several of the sisters joined us, and often either one or two of them brought their guitars. Most of the sisters had beautiful voices. I loved it when we sang songs. I especially loved it when the sisters led us and directed us to harmonize. One song I remember is, "Michael, row your boat ashore, alleluia ..." We could sing songs all night as far as I was concerned. We sometimes roasted marshmallows, or the sisters passed around goodies.

Shoreham Built New Cottages

As I got older, the camp was remodeled, and the Big House was no longer used for sleeping. New cottages were built in light green, yellow, white, and light blue. The main building was used for recreation, the sisters' quarters, Mass, the infirmary, eating meals, and parties.

To wind down the night, all the girls were brought to the dining room for a bedtime snack. We knew we had fifteen minutes to eat. Then Sister announced, "It's time to go to your cottage and get prepared for bed."

We lined up as the counselors took attendance, and we headed off to our cabins.

Each cottage housed six to eight girls. A sister and a counselor were assigned to our cottage to facilitate our movement. The sisters stayed with us, and the counselors had their own cabin. We picked up our toothbrush and towel and then went down to the bathhouse. There were rows of shower stalls, a row of sinks, and bathroom stalls. The counselor inside the bathhouse assisted us in moving along. We went back to the cottage as a group, put on our pajamas, and settled down. Sister said night prayers, then let us know that we had five minutes to be in bed under the covers before the lights went out. A favorite memory is waking up to the bugle playing "Reveille." We jumped out of bed and were dressed and ready to go to the bathhouse to wash up.

Because the summer cottages had been built, we learned a new song. It was exciting to learn and sing it at our campfire sing-alongs, and I never forgot the first verse, "Shoreham has new cottages,

cottages, cottages. Shoreham has new cottages. They're painted green, yellow, white and blue ..." We identified the cottage we slept in by its color.

We always went to church on Sunday, and at camp, Mass was set up in the recreation room so we were able to fit. I loved being at Mass with everyone in the camp. It was even better when I finally made my First Holy Communion. I often experienced being close to God. We were always reminded of how much God loves us, and I believed it.

Every year, when our month at camp came to a close and we had to return to St. Joseph's Hall, I felt sad. It was never easy for me to leave. I usually cried for the first twenty minutes of packing. Getting in line to board the bus for the long ride back to Brooklyn was difficult.

What I learned from my camp experience is how much I love the country. Summer at camp was a time when I felt loved and wanted and cared for by the sisters. No matter what my circumstances were at the time, I learned that keeping a positive attitude helped me realize that I mattered. This experience exposed me to the country and to loving, caring people around me.

Other Fond Memories in the Orphanage

Being in the orphanage was all I knew. I learned to accept my life. I also learned to put others first. I grew up to be a kind, giving person. I did miss my mother and father very much, but I knew they couldn't take care of me. The orphanage staff planned many fun times for us children to enjoy.

Every year, during the Christmas holidays, we went to Gimbels Department Store in New York City on Thirty-Fourth Street. For a few hours, they closed the toy department for us. The store manager said, "Girls, pick one toy or doll you want for Christmas."

I was thrilled. I once picked out a Raggedy Ann doll. It was my favorite doll.

Afterward, they had a special lunch for us. It was a memorable day.

Another fun event was when people put on plays for us. Once my sister June was in *The Music Man*. It was another great day.

We were also taken to fun places, such as the circus and the zoo. I loved seeing all the animals. Before our visits to the zoo, I had only seen such animals on television—the few times we watched television.

Once a year, we were taken to Steeplechase Park, which was an amusement park in the Coney Island area of Brooklyn. We had so much fun. The park was open just for us. I remember going down this wide, scary slide, where we had to put a safety blanket under us. Once I went down the slide successfully, I wanted to do it again and again. We had popcorn, cotton candy, hotdogs, and french fries at the park. Another great day.

As I said before, I had many good times in the orphanage. I shared a few here to show that, for me, life at St. Joseph's was all I knew. and I was often happy. I admit, emotionally, there were times I missed my parents and wished I had parents who cared about me. But since I was three years old when I entered the orphanage, my relationship with God shaped my experience and my life.

Visits with My Parents

Usually for Christmas, Easter, and Thanksgiving, my sisters and I were able to go home for the day with one of our parents. When my father and Uncle Sydney came to visit, they sometimes took us out for the day. They either brought my sisters and me to visit with Aunt Nettie and Uncle Leon or Aunt Jessie and Uncle Hyme. We sometimes got to see our cousins, and that was special. Those were peaceful and joyful visits. Whenever my father could, he brought us new dresses, coats, hats, and shoes for the occasion. Whenever he did that for us, it gave me a feeling of belonging.

When my mother took us home, usually Jimmy, my stepfather, picked us up with the car. When I met my stepfather, Jimmy, for the first time, I was about five years old. He was very Italian looking, with black hair and a mustache. He was a little taller than my mother and thin. He seemed nice. I first met my half sister Maryann, who was five years younger than me, maybe a few months old. She was tiny and adorable with dark hair and big brown eyes.

I usually didn't enjoy being at my mother's apartment, especially when she and Jimmy started drinking. There was often yelling, and it bothered me.

The best part of visiting was getting to be with my sisters for the day. I was happy when I returned to the orphanage, but I felt sad that I had to leave my little sister, Maryann, behind.

Chapter 5

Being in a Catholic orphanage run by the Sisters of Charity at the age of three made a huge impression on me. Knowing I was an orphan needing childcare and that the sisters took care of me because of their dedication to God touched my heart. In our home, there were many statues of saints. When I got older, I realized I lived in a religious house, and it was what helped me feel safe all those years. I always had this childlike faith throughout my life. My years in the orphanage taught me about selfless giving and service to others for the glory of God. Not every girl had this religious experience, but I did. I was blessed.

At the orphanage, we had a huge church in the middle of the first floor. It was beautiful, with statues all around. We had statues of St. Elizabeth Ann Seton, St. Vincent De Paul, St. Anthony of Padua, St. Teresa the Little Flower, St. Frances of Assisi, and many other saints. I wanted to know and learn more about each of them. My religious life was formed through the lives of the saints and the sisters I lived with. Often, Sister would have a movie (on a large screen) about one of these saints. I remember seeing the *Song of Bernadette* and *St. Teresa*, an ordinary girl, extraordinary soul, and I wanted to be just like them. Another favorite of mine was *Miracle of Marcelino.* This little boy lost his mother at a very young age and was raised by monks. It was a story that touched my heart deeply. So, at age seven, I was ready to prepare myself for my First Holy Communion.

Ruth Hostak

The Happiest Day of My Life

I received my First Holy Communion on May 12, 1957, at age seven, at St. Joseph's Hall Chapel. This was the happiest day of my life. My father bought me a beautiful white dress, white veil, white shoes, and bag. My bouquet of flowers was gorgeous. I felt so special and happy. I knew God loved me. We had much preparation for First Holy Communion. We met each day to learn our prayers and to understand what receiving the Eucharist meant. We learned the Eucharist was the body of Christ Jesus. Of course, at age seven, I had no idea how that could be, since we were receiving a wafer in our mouth, but I always loved God, so it didn't matter. If the saints and sisters believed it was the body of Christ, I was willing to believe. We were taught that when we receive the Holy Communion in our mouth, we do not chew it. We must allow it to dissolve and swallow it. I thought that sounded simple.

We were taught how to go to confession and why it was important. We learned that going to confession was special because Jesus forgives our sins through the priest. Father then gives us a blessing. We also learned that going to confession is called a sacrament of penance. It imparts divine grace. We have to be sorry and be willing to try not to sin again.

My first confession was frightening. I had no idea if the priest was going to yell at me or not. I had the usual sins of a seven-year-old. I disobeyed Sister, got mad at another girl. I didn't do my homework. The sin I was most afraid to tell was that, when I had a chance, I stole pretzels from the closet. I knew that when I confessed that sin, I could never do it again, because Father knew about it. He was kind and reminded me that Jesus forgives me and loves me. It wasn't scary at all. Father gave me several Hail Mary's and the Our Father to say, and I didn't mind doing that. I loved to pray.

We often were given the opportunity to go to church in the morning with the sisters. After seeing the story of Bernadette and St. Teresa, I couldn't wait to go to Mass whenever I was allowed. Sister told us if we wanted to go to Mass in the morning and be with the Lord, to tie a sock on the foot of our bed, and she would wake us up. I loved going to church in the morning. It made me feel special, and, also, I loved watching the sisters receiving the Holy Communion.

The big day came. I looked and felt beautiful. My dress was silk, with elegant tucks on the bodice and lined in soft 100 percent cotton. It was covered with layered ruffles. My veil was just as beautiful. All the girls looked beautiful and radiant in their white dresses. I couldn't wait to receive Jesus. We walked into the church and down the aisle, two by two. My sisters, June and Annie, were in the back of the church with my daddy. It made me smile to see them. But I didn't see my mother. The Mass began, and instead of paying attention to the priest and getting my heart ready to receive Jesus, I kept looking in the back of the church for my mother. Finally, she showed up, and I was able to concentrate on my love for Jesus. Before I knew it, it was time to receive Holy Communion. Remembering what the sisters taught me about Jesus made this experience exciting. As I kneeled at the altar, I started feeling butterflies in my stomach. I was next, and the priest placed on my tongue the wafer, the body of Christ. I went back to my seat, remembering Sister saying, "Do not chew the host." But, oh my, it got stuck on the roof of my mouth. I used my tongue to try to get it down, but it wasn't working. I was not sure what to do. It scared me because I did not want to commit a sin the first time, I received the host. Eventually, I was able to loosen it and swallow it. Thank God. I swallowed Jesus, and it wasn't easy, but it made me happy. I was now just like the sisters. I could go to Mass and receive Jesus. That was all I could think about. When Mass was over, we went out of the church (in pairs once again) and into the arms of my mother, father, and sisters.

My father spent time with us taking pictures. I hated having my picture taken because the sun was always in my eyes, but this was a special day, so I tried to smile.

Mother and Ruthie—First Holy Communion day

My father took us to my mother's apartment. He came in for a short time and left. I met my half sister Connie, one or two months old. She was adorable. Connie was a bundle of joy with chubby cheeks. Maryann was two years old at the time. I loved spending time with them. Looking back, I remember this day as being one of the most peaceful days at my mother's apartment. Jimmy was a great Italian cook. When he started cooking, the smells in the kitchen were so yummy that my nostrils were filled with garlic, parsley, onions, and the gravy sauce itself. He made a delicious dinner for us, consisting of Italian meatballs, sausage, and pieces of pork and beef with rigatoni pasta and ricotta cheese. It was a treat. The best part of my visit was that I got to play with Maryann and Connie. It was difficult to say goodbye to my little sisters. I felt so many different emotions and sadness that I had to leave them.

Throughout the years, whenever I told a story about my orphanage years, I always said I was seven years of age. I realize this was one of the most memorable years of my life. Receiving Holy Communion had a huge impact on me. It changed my life for the better. It helped me to form a deeper connection with Jesus. This connection served me well during my last two years in the orphanage.

Chapter 6

I was packing for summer camp when I heard the news that I was going home for good. Instead of being excited, my thoughts were, *I wish I could go home after summer camp.* Summer camp was my favorite time of the year, and I was going to be deprived of it. Oh, well. I had a lump in my stomach, and I was terrified thinking about not being at St. Joseph's anymore. I felt safe and comfortable being with the sisters. I had no idea what was in store for me at home. The only experience I had being at home was when my mother had permission to take us home for the day. I was happy to be with my little sisters, but I didn't enjoy the bad behavior of my mother and stepfather, especially when they were drinking. I did love my mother and felt happy she finally wanted me.

Going Home for Good

Getting ready to go home for good was a process. I was nine years of age. Annie was twelve, and June was thirteen. Annie and June were happy and couldn't wait to go home. It was a mixed bag for me. I was happy, but I was sad and disappointed that I had to miss summer camp.

I needed to say my goodbyes before I left. I first went to Sister Michael, who managed the kitchen and the laundry room. I entered her office to tell her the news.

She asked, "Ruthie, how do you feel about going home?"

I told her, "I wish I could go to summer camp first."

She gave me a big smile.

I told her I was happy my mother wanted me now and could take carc of me, but I was terrified of the unknown.

Sister gave me encouragement.

As tears ran down my face, I told Sister Michael I was going to miss her a lot. She gave me a big hug.

"I promise to pray for you, Ruthie. You will do well," she said.

Sister Michael was one of my favorite sisters and always showed she cared. She said, "Ruthie, tell the women in the laundry room that you are going home. I know they would like to say goodbye."

I had often volunteered to bring the weekly sheets down to the laundry room, and I always said good morning to each of the women as I passed by to hand in the sheets in the back of the room. Often, one of them would give me a lollipop or a cookie. There were about ten ladies who worked in the laundry room. They fixed our clothing that needed repair, and they took care of the laundry. They each had a table with a sewing machine on it, one behind the other in a long row on the right side of the room. Then the big machines were in the back.

When I arrived in the laundry room and told Lucy, my favorite lady, I was going home for good, she gave me a big hug and a jar. Lucy put a dollar in the jar and said, "Let each of the ladies know you are going home for good. I am sure they each want to give you a gift."

I did not expect money from them. They were so kind.

I had to say goodbye to Sister Joseph, so I went up to where I knew she would be and, of course, I ran into her arms. I told her I was going home for good. She hugged me tight and said she was so happy for me. I told her I was scared.

She said, "Ruthie, it is okay to be scared, but just know I will be praying for you. I know you will do well, and your mother is so excited to have you home."

Sister Joseph already knew I was going home since she was in charge of the units. I experienced grief and fear of letting go, knowing I would never see her again. She was like a mother to me. I didn't want her to see me cry, but when I walked away, I couldn't hold it in any longer. I cried my eyes out.

All the girls in my division were happy and excited for me. Going home for good was a big deal. Sister provided a cake, balloons, and candy, and the girls prepared a song to sing to me. It only made me feel worse that I was leaving an environment I had learned to love.

Annie and June were beyond excited. They couldn't wait to go home. They both were ready to leave the minute they were told we were leaving.

We all had an exit interview. I don't remember much of it. I do remember my mother in the waiting room, waiting for us to leave. I ran into the chapel and asked the Blessed Mother to watch over me as I returned home. My sisters and my mother waited patiently for me, and off we went, leaving behind the only home I ever felt safe in and entering the next phase of my life.

As we walked out the door and down the block, just before we crossed the street, I remember thinking how much I wished I could run back and stay with the sisters. But I said to myself, *Ruthie, you can't go back. You don't want Mom to think you don't love her.* My heart ached. But I kept walking away from the orphanage, never to return.

My stepfather was waiting down the next street in the car to take us to our new apartment.

Chapter 7

Living on Flushing Avenue

We arrived at Flushing Avenue, Brooklyn, New York. My little sisters were being watched by my mother's next-door neighbor, Miss Fink. She was the babysitter for my younger sisters while both of our parents worked. This particular day, they both had taken off from work to pick us up.

We all packed into the car, and after a short ride, we arrived at our new home. I was not excited. I was more fearful than anything else. We lived on the second floor of the building. We had four rooms and a bathroom. They were railroad rooms. We obtained heat in the apartment from a short black pot belly stove. My step-father filled it with coal, and it provided heat. It was in the back bedroom where my mom and stepfather slept. There was also a big hot water tank in the kitchen, and we needed to light a match to heat it up. It also warmed up the kitchen and gave us hot water for the dishes and to take a bath or wash up in the bathroom. In the winter, the room I slept in wasn't warm enough, but as long as I stayed under the covers, it was good enough to sleep. If I got up to go to the bathroom, I shivered until I was safely back under the covers again. I slept with my sister Annie, and June slept on a folding bed next to us. Annie shook herself to sleep as I lay awake until she stopped shaking. During the day, June's bed folded up. It was replaced by the television. The bed I slept in with Annie was covered and used as a couch. The room next to our room was small, and it was perfect for Connie and Maryann. The kitchen was medium size with two windows. The windows were dressed with brightly colored light green curtains. The table had a matching tablecloth. The small apartment was cluttered. Everything was in its place when I first arrived home, but that was the only time I remember it being neat and clean.

After we settled in, Mother called Ms. Fink and my sisters in from next door. Ms. Fink had gray hair and was a heavy woman. Connie ran into my arms. She was so cute and adorable with big brown eyes and brown hair. At this time, she was two years old. I loved to be with her. Maryann was precious. She was four. She ran to Annie. In the beginning, it felt great having all five siblings together. My mother introduced us to Ms. Fink, who lived next door and let us know that she took care of Maryann and Connie Monday through Friday.

My mother was busy working, cooking, and being with my stepfather. Very rarely did she show any interest in me.

Often, Friday nights were very late nights. Usually, Mother's friends came to the apartment to play cards and drink. I did enjoy watching them play cards until I became tired and went to bed. But until they left the apartment, it wasn't easy to sleep. They drank and played cards until the wee hours of the morning.

On the weekends, Jimmy often made our Sunday meal. We often had my favorite Italian food. I looked forward to Sundays. When I awoke, I could often tell the gravy was cooking. It filled my nostrils with such great smells.

I was the only one who went to church on Sunday. I walked to Saint Leonard's Roman Catholic Church alone. I was glad my mother let me go. I knew I was going to be with Jesus, so I didn't mind going by myself. I was nine years of age, but I felt older. I felt close to God when I was in church. It helped me feel connected to a life I was used to while growing up in the orphanage. I felt a deep connection. Going home from church, I was happy and joyful, and sometimes I skipped. Usually, when I arrived home, I was happy to play with my little sisters. Since I didn't see them much during the week, it was fun to be with them on the weekends.

I tried my best to stay out of the way in our small apartment. There were five of us girls at home at once, and it was crowded. The summer was upon us, so I was off from school. It was hot in our apartment, so when I could, I went outside. I liked to walk around the neighborhood. I also enjoyed going to the store for my mother. She left money and a list on the table, and I went to the local grocery store. My favorite store was Levy's day-old bakery. The store sold more than cake. It also had day-old bread and doughnuts. Mother let me know what she wanted, then let me pick out either doughnuts or a cake. I enjoyed being able to choose.

A few times during the summer, when Jimmy and my mother were off from work, we were taken on a picnic. It was so much fun being in the park and running around. I loved playing with my two little sisters.

Jimmy also took us to visit my grandmother and grandfather who lived in Rocky Point, Long Island, New York. We left early in the morning and returned home late at night. I loved visiting with my grandmother. She was so loving. My grandfather was scary. He only spoke Italian and wasn't friendly. I rarely saw them, so the times I did were a treat.

The difficult part of being home with Jimmy and my mother was when they didn't get along. It often happened in the evening or on weekends. It was painful when I had to listen to them screaming and yelling. I became protective of my younger sisters. I took them to the back room and tried to ignore my mother and stepfather.

Attending Public School for the First Time

In September, I went to Public School 145. I entered the fourth grade. I had completed the third grade in the orphanage. My mother's neighbor Lorraine Smith took me to register for school since my mother couldn't miss work. Lorraine lived upstairs from us and was kind and caring. I had butterflies in my stomach the first day of school and many days after. It was hard being in an environment with girls and boys I did not know. I didn't make friends easily. I cringed with fear, and my heart pounded in my chest the first few weeks. Being around boys felt strange to me. I trembled being near them. I had no idea how to relate to boys. They seemed different. I knew I had to get used to school, but I also knew it wasn't going to be easy.

In the beginning, I couldn't wait until the school day was over and I was out the door. I didn't speak to anyone. If someone asked me a question, I answered as quickly as I could. Eventually, I met Susan, who reached out and made me feel comfortable. One day, Susan said, "Ruthie, where do you live?"

I said, "Flushing Avenue."

She responded, "We live in the same direction. Let's walk home together." I enjoyed our friendship, and it made school more bearable.

In the morning, I walked to school by myself. It was about six blocks from our apartment. One time, toward the end of November, I left for school, and it was freezing cold outside. The sky was overcast with clouds, and chilly winds were blowing. I shivered as I began my walk to school. The temperature was around thirty-five degrees. My mother said, "Ruthie, I am sorry I don't have the money to buy you a coat. I get paid at the end of the week, and then I will buy you one."

Mother suggested I wear two sweaters, so I did, but it was still cold. The teacher reported me to the guidance counselor. I was called out of the classroom, and the guidance counselor escorted me into her office. She asked me a lot of questions. She then asked me why I didn't wear a coat coming to school. I explained that my mother had to wait for her paycheck before she could buy me a coat. The counselor then took me into a room with some coats hanging on a rack, and she gave me a really pretty blue one. I had a big smile because it was pretty and warm. She said, "Ruthie, when the school day is over, come to my office to pick up your coat."

I thanked her and went back to class.

Becoming a Girl Scout

Once, when walking home, Susan told me she was a Girl Scout. She asked me if I wanted to go with her to a meeting. I promised I'd ask my mother and let her know the next day. To my surprise, my mother said yes, and I was excited.

The meetings were on Fridays, after dinner. Susan met me at my apartment, and off we went to the Girl Scout meeting. As we walked, we sometimes skipped to a meeting. We made up a song, and we both sang it along the way. It went like this: "2-811 when I die, I will go to heaven." Our Girl Scout troop number was 2-811. Attending the meetings was fun. The girls were friendly. I learned the oath, "On my honor, I will try to do my duty, to help others in need, to serve God and my country, and remember the girl scout law." We discussed topics such as confidence, character, and leadership. We were planning on several events, community service, learning first aid, and earning badges by acquiring practical skills. When I was going to become an official member, I asked my mother for the money for my uniform, and she informed me that she didn't have extra money and that we were moving in a few months anyway. It was a big disappointment.

When I got home from school, most days it was peaceful. I usually went straight to the back room, flopped onto my mother's bed, and did my homework or took a nap. One of my favorite pastimes was sitting by the window, counting the cars. I played little games with myself, counting colors of the cars or looking for a letter, starting with A and ending with Z. It relaxed me. Once my mother came home and the two little ones came in from next door, a lot of screaming took place. I enjoyed playing with my sisters. But I didn't enjoy the screaming. Mother was self-involved much of the time. Very rarely did she show any interest in me. I don't remember her once asking me how my day went at school.

I rarely had new clothes. My mother had five girls, and I was in the middle. Either my older sisters or the two younger ones received new clothes when my mother could afford it. Otherwise, my stepfather, Jimmy, worked in a rag company sorting donations. Many times, he brought home bags of clothes, and we made a run for them. If I grabbed something that was too big, it went to my older sisters. Often, I liked what Jimmy brought home. I knew that my mother had five of us to feed and couldn't also afford new clothes. I appreciated whatever Jimmy bought home.

Uncle Sydney's Surprise visit on my 10th Birthday

One significant experience on Flushing Avenue was on my tenth birthday. Uncle Sydney came to visit me. I loved and missed him. He called my mother and received permission to visit. When he rang the bell, I went running down the stairs. I hadn't seen him since I returned from the orphanage.

For my birthday, Uncle Sydney took me to the ice-cream parlor in the neighborhood. I had a hamburger and French fries, then a big dish of vanilla ice cream. He asked me how I was doing in school. He was the first person besides the guidance counselor at school who asked me how I was doing. He was interested in me, and I felt loved. Then Uncle Sydney gave me a birthday gift that brought joy to my heart and a big smile to my face. It was a big jar of quarters, dimes, nickels, and pennies. I thought, *He must have been saving all year.*

For some reason, which I never knew, Uncle Sydney was not allowed to come upstairs to our apartment. He helped me upstairs with the big jar and left before I opened the door. I felt sad when he said goodbye. I had the jar of money for what seemed like years. I put it in a secret hiding place. Whenever I wanted candy, I took some of the change from the jar and recalled how much my uncle Sydney loved me.

My mother did not live for her children. She didn't have the skills needed to be a good, caring mother. She preferred working and being out of the apartment. For years, I craved my mother's touch. I waited for Mom to reach out to me. But that act of tenderness rarely came. I was used to being pushed aside and verbally put down. Most of the time, I made sure I stayed out of her way. On weekends, as long as my parents had friends over to play cards, they were not fighting with each other. At other times, my stepfather squandered the bulk of his earnings on drinking and gambling. He liked betting with a bookie or at the track. I rarely felt safe at home. I turned to God for comfort, belonging, and support.

Confirmation Day

In order to receive my Confirmation, I had to get permission from my mother, and she was happy to give it. I needed a godmother for Confirmation. Since I didn't know anyone to ask, I had to rely on my mother. She asked Lorraine Smith, the neighbor who had enrolled me into school in September. I also needed to decide on a name for my Confirmation. My mother gave me the name Lorraine to honor her friend.

Lorraine was a nice lady. She also was a churchgoer. I was ten years of age when I went to religious instructions to learn about the Holy Spirit. I loved being in church. It was where I felt safe and loved by God. I went to religious instructions weekly for several months in preparation to be confirmed.

During religious instructions, I learned that through Confirmation the Holy Spirit would give me an increased ability to practice my Catholic faith. I was enthusiastic to learn more about Confirmation as a sacrament. It was a Christian initiation into the Catholic Church. I was eager to receive Confirmation. My mother was also joyful that I was going to be confirmed. She had a deep faith in God but didn't practice her religion, although sometimes she prayed for God's help in her life. She told me she looked forward to attending my Confirmation and would be proud to do so. I was happy that she cared about my spiritual life, even a little.

Finally, the preparation for Confirmation was completed. It was time to get ready for my big day. My father bought me a beautiful light green dress. I also wore a white Confirmation gown. I loved that Daddy knew receiving my Confirmation was an important day and wanted to buy my dress. I realized it was his way of expressing his love. June and Annie came to the church with mother. My stepfather stayed home with my two little sisters and began preparing a wonderful Italian feast to celebrate. I walked down the aisle, with Lorraine by my side, and we entered a pew together. My mother and my two sisters stayed in the back of the church. June took pictures.

Our bishop shared, "The Holy Spirit will fill your hearts today, and that is a gift and a blessing."

I was really happy. I had looked forward to this special day.

Each of us formed a line with our sponsor by our side. One at a time, we were in front of the bishop. Chills moved through my body as we approached him.

First was the laying on of hands. The bishop placed his hands on my head. Then he made the sign of the cross on my forehead while saying my confirmation name, Lorraine. Then the bishop anointed my forehead with oil. A warmth enveloped my body, and I knew the Holy Spirit was present.

When all the girls had received Confirmation, His Excellency asked us to renew our baptismal promises. We repeated after him a beautiful prayer, renewed our baptismal promises, and we were confirmed. The bishop blessed all the sponsors and thanked them for being part of our lives.

After church, my sister June took pictures of me and my sponsor, me, my mother, and Annie. I felt proud and happy that I had received the Holy Spirit to guide my life. When we arrived back to our apartment building and were on the stairs, I smelled Italian gravy and knew we were in for a delicious dinner.

When Annie and I did the house cleaning, we often sang in

harmony the confirmation song I learned and taught her. It goes like this: "I am a soldier in Christ's army, Confirmation made it so, I am a solider in Christ's army, I profess my faith wherever I go, oh the devil shall not harm me, for God's the captain of my soul ..."

Annie and I enjoyed singing songs together.

What I learned from my Confirmation was that the Holy Spirit wants to guide my day, if I ask. It has served me most of my life. Even today, a favorite prayer is "Holy Spirit, please lead my day." Then the rest of my day is peaceful because I realize that whatever I do during the day, I am serving God.

Chapter 8

Shortly after Confirmation, my mother informed me that we were moving to Greenpoint, Brooklyn, New York. I was terrified of moving since Flushing Avenue was the only apartment I had lived in since my days in the orphanage.

We moved to 148 Kingsland Avenue, Brooklyn, New York, into a much larger apartment. We lived one flight up on the first floor. The building was well lit and clean. The rooms were railroad, but there were more of them. I walked into a large living room, and then to the right was a large kitchen, but the bathroom was rather small. The window in the bathroom led on to a roof that was attached to the next building. We often went on the roof. We hung our laundry on the roof to dry. Sometimes in the summer, when it was so hot and I could hardly breathe, I made my bed outside the window and slept on the roof. Sometimes my sisters and I hung out on the roof during the day since the apartment was too hot.

To the left of the living room were the bedrooms. The first bedroom was large and fit two large beds and several wardrobes and dressers. My sister Annie and I shared a bed, and my sisters Connie and Maryann shared the bed next to us. Each room had a window since we lived in a corner apartment. The next bedroom was small and only fit a bed and a dresser. My older sister June had that room. Her wardrobe was in our room. My mother and stepfather had the back room. It had three windows. Their room was on the corner. It was a big, open space. I enjoyed going to their room when they were working. I would hang out by myself and do my homework, read a romance novel, or listen to music.

One of the biggest complaints about living in this apartment was the roaches. At night, I hated to go into the bathroom. I turned on the light, and hundreds of roaches scattered. I was totally appalled by the disgusting hygiene in the bathroom. Whenever I wanted to take a shower, I had to first clean the bathtub. No one in the apartment cleaned up after themselves. It was the one thing about living on Kingsland Avenue that I despised. No one put their things away. From the oldest to the youngest, they were all slobs. My sister Annie and I mostly cleaned the apartment. Once in a while, Mother would be on a rampage and have us all help clean. She was frantic and threw away anything that was in the way. I loved when the whole apartment was clean and neat, but it never stayed that way for long.

One joyful memory I have back then is of me and Annie singing songs as we cleaned. One favorite song we often sang was the Ten Commandments. We each took a verse and sang it. "First, I must honor God, second honor His name, third on His day keep holy this will be my aim. Fourth, I must be obedient, fifth be kind and true, sixth, be pure in all I say and see and hear and do, seventh I must be honest, eighth, be truthful in all things I say, ninth, be pure in mind and heart and all I think and desire each day, tenth, I must be satisfied, not be jealous come what may. These are God's Ten Commandments. These I must obey." Singing religious songs helped us get through the cleaning and made it fun.

June, Annie, and I had assigned chores since Mother worked all day. My job was doing the dinner dishes and keeping the sink clean, especially since the roaches roamed around the kitchen at night. I didn't mind doing the dishes. Sometimes if I was in a rush to go outside and meet my friends, I traded with Annie, and she did the dishes for me. I often couldn't wait to get the dishes done.

I loved hanging out with my two friends that lived across the street. Yet I never felt safe sharing my hurt feelings with them for fear of rejection. We often hung out on the church steps or at the candy store. We had fun together. There were other girls who joined us. We often hung out wherever the boys were. One or more of the boys usually had a crush on one of my friends, and some of the girls had a crush on the boys. Most of the times, the boys interacted with us by teasing us. Usually, one boy would tease someone he liked. It was a silly way of relating, but they were young and inexperienced. The boys were very protective of us, and sometimes one or two of them walked us home.

Sometimes I went to Italian Marie's apartment to listen to music. She was a genuine friend. She and I had fun together, and it was obvious she cared. One time, her grandmother died, and they laid her out in the living room. Seeing her in the living room in a coffin scared the living daylights out of me. But I acted brave to support Marie because she was so sad. Her grandmother was a wonderful person and often invited me to eat lunch with them.

The storefronts downstairs in our building included a restaurant and an Italian men's social club. I enjoyed spending time looking out the window. I loved watching the activity. On the weekends, I enjoyed sitting outside with the neighbors, watching all the people come and go. Often, especially in the summer, many of our neighbors took chairs outside and sat in front of their building or on their stoop for hours. Some played cards on card tables till the wee hours of the morning. During the summer, the block was always packed with neighbors. Since it was hot in the apartments, and not everyone could afford air-conditioning, they enjoyed the company outside.

In September, I started attending PS 110. I was put into the sixth grade. The first few weeks of school, I had butterflies in my stomach. Once I became comfortable, I survived the year with few problems. I attended this school for one year. One awkward experience I had was when the nurse from the dentist's office came into my classroom and asked me to go with her to see the dentist. I thought I would die when she pulled me out of class. We all knew that only poor students saw the dentist at school. Some of the kids made fun of me when I returned, and it hurt.

Every Wednesday at two o'clock, my teacher, Ms. Ford, dismissed all Catholic students to attend religious instruction. We lined up on the right side of the classroom, and when the bell rang, we were dismissed. I attended St. Cecelia's Church. It was the highlight of my week.

June quit school since she was sixteen and started working. Annie often stayed home from school and at one point was put into a detention center for a month for missing too many days of school. She told me it was a frightening experience. The girls were mean and tried to pick fights with her. It upset me that she was punished for staying home, taking care of my two little sisters, Maryann and Connie, when the babysitter wasn't available, which was often.

When ready for the seventh grade, I attended John Ericson Junior High School 126. I had a positive attitude toward school and wanted to learn. I promised myself I would not be like my sisters. I would do whatever was necessary to graduate from school. But I had a lot of emotional problems, and it was tough for me to concentrate in class. I did try my best. Because of my emotional problems, I constantly fell asleep in class. Sometimes teachers just let me sleep; other times, a teacher would say loudly, "Ruth, wake up and pay attention." This embarrassed me.

Mother left the house early in the morning to go to work. It was up to us to get ourselves to school, and I always did. But Mother never took an interest in how I was doing in school. She knew I was going, and that was good enough. She never came for open-school week. She needed to work.

My mother's friend Betty was often around. When she could, she babysat Maryann and Connie. Whenever I was sick and needed to go to the doctor, Betty took me to the clinic and sat with me for hours. I frequently developed sore throats, and sometimes Dr. Chiffo was available a few blocks from our apartment. When my mother had money, I went by myself to his office for a checkup and antibiotics.

Ruth Hostak

The Death of Uncle Sydney

I was around thirteen when I found out my Uncle Sydney died. Sadly, I didn't get to say goodbye. I cried myself to sleep that night. Uncle Sydney had been a loving, caring uncle. My mother explained that in the Jewish tradition, a person is buried the very next day. I missed him so much. For days after Uncle Sydney died, I felt grief and heartache knowing I would never see him again.

At home, I felt emotionally unseen by my mother. I was not emotionally responded to as a teenager. It was a lonely experience. I never felt wanted. I felt alone in the world. I had a gut feeling of emptiness. I looked for affection from my mother, but often she couldn't be bothered. If I reached out to her, she would let me, but I never remembered her reaching out to me. Hence, it took years for me to learn how to reach out to others. I had to learn how to relate to people on my own.

My mother was a lining maker in a coat factory. She did piecework. She got paid for how many linings she finished in a day. Whenever she had the opportunity to make more money, she worked late. She loved working and making money. Yet, whenever I asked her for money for school or anything else, her response was "I'm broke. Ask your father."

My father didn't live with us, and I only saw him when I had to collect Mother's money for the week. When I asked my father for money, he tried to give me something, if he had it, but it wasn't much. Other times, I just hoped he would offer me some money. My father spent a lot of his money on liquor, so on several occasions he would be broke. Frequently, when I went to visit him, I smelled liquor on his breath. I never felt comfortable. He wanted me to sit on his lap, but I did not trust him when he was drunk. I didn't like him touching me, and I was afraid of his affection.

One time, I had holes in my shoes. I showed my father that I needed money for shoes, and he gave me ten dollars to buy new shoes. I was limited with what I could buy since I didn't have much money. I went to the shoe store by myself. After the shoe salesman helped me with numerous pairs of shoes, I chose a pair that were too tight. I was embarrassed to leave the store without buying a pair of shoes. Eventually, I had to bring them to the shoemaker to get them stretched. But they never fit right. The lesson I learned was never go to the shoe store without someone else to be my advocate.

McCarren Park happened to be in the neighborhood. I enjoyed spending time in the park whenever I wanted to get out of the house and my friends were not around. I would sit on a bench and watch people go by. While at the park, I figured out a way to make some money. Soda bottles had a deposit of five cents. I watched people throw their soda bottles in the garbage pails, and I thought, *Wow! I could make enough money for candy.* I carried a big plastic bag with me to the park and collected the soda bottles and took them to the candy store across from the park. It was a fun thing to do, and I received a refund and either bought candy or kept some change for another time.

Once, Mother asked me to get something out of her pocketbook. As I opened it, I was shocked to see how much change and dollar bills she had accumulated. It bothered me that she always told me she was broke, yet I found all this money in her bag. Another time, when everyone was sleeping, I went into Mother's pocketbook and took some of the change. I decided she would never miss it since she had so much. I took change from her bag several times, when I wanted something and she wouldn't give it to me. I justified taking the money by believing it was okay since I needed it for school. All my friends received an allowance for the week, and I never did. They had money for a snack at lunchtime or a soda, and I had no money for anything and had to eat the school lunch. I felt sad and embarrassed to not have money like my friends did. Sometimes they offered me a snack or a soda, and that felt good.

I have to admit that as soon as Mother got paid, she filled the refrigerator with fruits, vegetables, and other produce. Unfortunately, by the time the middle of the week rolled around, it was mostly gone.

I look back on this experience now and realize that my mother had five of us to feed. It wasn't easy. She had to prioritize her money. I finally understood she did the best she could.

Mother had a sewing machine at home, and every now and then she would say, "Bring anything that needs to be sewed, fixed, or hemmed, and I will do it for you."

Jimmy continued to bring used clothing home, and much of it needed to be altered.

When in the ninth grade, I took a typing class. I loved typing. One Christmas, my mother surprised me with a Royal portable typewriter. She knew I loved typing because I constantly talked about it to anyone who would listen, and Mother heard me. The typewriter was one of the biggest surprises of my life. I was so overjoyed; it was Mother's way of expressing her love for me, and I felt the love.

My first part-time job after school was typing up forms. I worked for various companies as a typist. I attribute part of my success in my early work life to my mother buying me the typewriter.

Another special time with my mother, during my teenage years, was when she taught me how to crochet. I enjoyed learning the skill. It wasn't until many years later that I took it up again. Even today, I crochet blankets, bookmarks, scarfs, and placemats. Most of my close friends and family members have received one of these gifts from me.

While in school, I had many challenges. I once wrote a short biography of my life for my English class. My English teacher, Mrs. Drummer, liked me and took an interest in me. She was supportive of me doing well in school. She often asked me to stay after classes and help her with projects. She encouraged me a lot. Once, she said, "Ruthie, reach for the stars, and you will succeed. Never give up on yourself. Remember you can do it."

I have never forgotten Mrs. Drummer's advice. It made a huge impact on my life. One of my best qualities throughout my life has been perseverance. I never give up on myself. I learned to look at what is in front of me and not look back. I also discovered that when I believe in myself, others will also believe in me, and this has truly been my experience throughout my life. I became aware that I am a strong woman and have potential to accomplish anything I set my mind on achieving.

I realized that going to school was important. In my heart, I believed that I was intelligent and bright if given the chance.

Bullied Once Again

We received free bus passes for school, but usually I walked to school, unless it was too cold or I was late. I hated taking the bus. The boys from the projects entered the bus a stop or two after me. Whenever I saw them, I became paralyzed with fear. I would shake. They bullied me every time. I tried to ignore them, but they were mean and poked fun at me. One time, a boy sat next to me and, out loud, made mean comments about my appearance, calling me "big nose" to his friends, as if I was not sitting there.

"What a big nose she has," he said.

He would also make fun of something I might be wearing.

I tried to ignore these boys, but sometimes it didn't work. One of them would purposely push me as I got off the bus. I hated this. It made me a fear-filled teenager.

Junior High School Assembly

One incident that affected my ability to take risks, or to express myself fully for many years, was in the junior high school assembly. We had assembly once a week. The entire school grade came together so the administrators could speak with us as a group. Once, I was given the opportunity to recite a scripture passage (Psalm 23:1–6, the Lord is my Shepherd) at assembly. I knew it well. I memorized it and felt good about having this opportunity. When I got on stage, I looked out into the audience, and all I could see was this group of boys right in the front row that often bullied me in class. I was paralyzed. I could not speak. I tried to relax by taking deep breaths, but nothing helped. Someone handed me the Bible, so I could read directly from it, but by this time, I was shaking and sweating and wanted to run far away from these boys. I ran back to my seat and just cried. From then on, I didn't trust that people would receive me well. I grew up being terrified of being judged and not being accepted. I held onto the belief that I was not good enough for many years.

Junior high school was a mixed bag. On the one hand, I enjoyed being a student. On the other hand, I didn't like the abuse I had to put up with by some students who bullied me.

When I was ready to graduate from junior high school, my father took me to buy a beautiful dress. It was light blue and very elegant, with a princess collar and sleeves. I loved being treated special. My mother got a special deal for free pictures, so she had the photographer take pictures of me and Annie.

I was always ashamed of being half-Jewish because Italian boys were mean and made fun of the Jews. My last name is Goldberg, but I told the neighborhood boys that my last name was Graziano, my mother's maiden name. It was graduation day, and my last name was the last thing on my mind. Graduating from junior high school meant I would be going to high school. I was proud of myself that I had made it through.

On the day of graduation, our class marched onto the stage. I had no idea the principal intended to call each name one at a time. When a name was called, the student was required to stand to be acknowledged.

As I looked out into the audience, I noticed several of the boys from the neighborhood that my friends and I hung out with at night. I almost died when my name was called. All I could hear was "Ruth Goldberg." Oh my God. I thought I would die.

From that day on, none of the boys in the neighborhood called me Ruthie. They called me Goldberg. It was their way of teasing me. But from where I was coming from, it was mean and hurtful.

When I was fourteen and in the ninth grade, many mornings before school, I attended daily mass at St. Cecelia's Church. I needed the Lord in my life. I struggled to cope with all my problems in school and at home. It was in church that I felt a sense of belonging. I sat in the same pew daily, and so did other parishioners. Often, we nodded at each other when entering the pew. I loved that acknowledgment. Father Jim was the parish priest, and he was young and handsome. He seemed very caring. I felt a deep sense of Christian charity and love around him. Every day, I prayed for my family and then asked God to send me a boyfriend who was a good person, had good parents, went to church on Sunday, went to college, and drove a car. This was my dream. I prayed for over two years. I didn't go to Mass every day for all that time, but I did go often. Sometimes I went every day for weeks and then not every day, depending on what was going on in my life at the time.

At fifteen, I met Joyce and her sister, Sophie. We became good friends. We were inseparable. I loved being with them. Their mother worked nights and wasn't around much. When I asked my mother if I could sleep over at their apartment on the weekend, she let me. I never gave her a reason not to trust me, but she didn't pay much attention to me anyway. At times like these, I was happy my mother was easy. Yet, I always wished she was interested in me. She never once asked me, "How are you doing?" or "Do you need anything?" My mother was blind to my needs. Her own agenda came first. I realized early on that I was on my own. I had to figure things out for myself.

I don't remember my mother giving her advice about anything important to me. Mother was never concerned with whether I did my homework, or how I was doing with my friends, or what time I came home, unless she was in a bad mood or needed something from me. Those times, she threatened to call my father if I was not home on time. I was afraid of my father, so I always came home when I was supposed to, whether or not Mother noticed.

My Mother usually let me do whatever I wanted, yet most of my friends had boundaries to follow given by their parents. I thought that when parents had boundaries for their children, it meant his or her parents loved and cared about their lives and how they turned out.

My mother and stepfather had toxic traits. They were self-centered. They didn't think about my needs or feelings. My mother didn't have boundaries for me that could have helped me to develop as a woman. She used manipulation to get what she wanted from me. And I never felt my efforts were good enough. I usually listened to her when she wanted something just to make her happy. For years, I craved my mother's touch. As I grew up, I waited for Mom to reach out to me. But that act of affection rarely came. I was used to being pushed aside.

I didn't like that I had no boundaries other than to clean the kitchen after dinner, or help Annie clean the house, or run errands for Mother.

Since I had no boundaries set for me, I never learned how to be assertive. I avoided conflict at all costs, and it took a long time to learn how to express myself. I kept my hurt feelings to myself and suffered quietly. I rarely confronted people. Hence, for years, if someone upset me or treated me wrong, the only way I could express my feelings was to write them a letter. It took years and many workshops to learn how to express myself verbally.

My home life wasn't easy. At this time, I enjoyed being with Joyce and Sophie. It was fun whenever we were together. We spent a lot of time at their apartment. I admired their clothes and wished I had them.

My sister June worked and had nice clothes. She had a lock on her closet and warned me not to wear her clothes. Whenever I thought there was something special at school, or Joyce and Sophie invited be to do something fun, I asked June to lend me one of her outfits. But she usually said no. June reminded me not to touch her clothes. She thought her closet was secure, but I knew how to open the lock. When I wanted to wear her clothes, I picked the lock and wore one of her pretty outfits and made sure it was back in her closet before she got home from work. She was much taller than me, so I had to roll up the skirt and cover it with the blouse.

Once, I was by myself in a discount store. I stole a bra and got caught. I felt embarrassed and devastated. The salesperson took the bra from me and told me to leave the store. I guess she felt bad for me. She didn't want to bring attention to me. I was grateful.

As I left the store, I remembered making a promise that I would never take anything that wasn't mine again. I made an oath. I also spoke to God and said, "Thank you for me not getting into trouble." After this experience, I understood that stealing wasn't right, no matter what the circumstances.

At home, both my mother and stepfather were weekend alcoholics—or whenever there was a holiday and Mom was off from work the next day, she went to the bar. Jimmy often went to the bar after work during the week and sometimes came home drunk. When he wasn't drinking, he was a nice person. I liked him then. But when he was drunk, he was a nasty drunk. Those times, I stayed far away from him.

Jimmy had an addiction to gambling. He squandered the bulk of his earnings on drinking and gambling, and there wasn't much left for the family. Yet one of Jimmy's better qualities was his cooking. Besides his delicious gravy, he made snails in a great Italian sauce. We had to use a straight pin or a toothpick to get the snail out of the shell.

My mother was also a good cook, when she cooked. She made excellent seafood dishes, especially around the holidays. She made fried shrimp, eel, filet, and so on. I loved her cooking. She also sometimes made Italian cookies or cakes that were so delicious.

A Struggle with My Parents

On a Friday, instead of coming home from work, Jimmy went off to the track and many times lost his entire paycheck. He came home drunk and began fighting with my mother. It was horrible to experience them fighting. She screamed and yelled and then threw him out of the apartment. One time, I was sleeping, and they were screaming and fighting so loud that I woke up. I peeked through the bottom of the door, so I could hear and see what they were saying and doing. It wasn't pleasant. It upset my stomach as I watched them fighting. I felt some kind of sick excitement that I never understood. Once he left the apartment, he was gone for a few days. Then, when he won at the track, he called my mother, she forgave him, and he was back home.

At least one night during the week, and on weekends, Mother had card parties. I loved watching them, especially on weekends when I could stay up late. Usually, the week games took place in my neighbor's upstairs apartment. We always had a game in our apartment on the weekends. My mother had some nice woman friends, and they all loved to gamble. When Mother wasn't playing cards on the weekends, she was at the bar. It bothered me that she rarely did anything with her girls.

Joyce and I continued to be friends, and we both went to Eli Whitney Vocational High School. She was studying to be a beautician. I didn't know what I wanted to become, but I knew I liked typing. After school, I often went to Joyce's apartment for a little while, and we did our homework together. I then went home for dinner and the dishes. Other times, Joyce and I got together in the evening to hang out with our friends. It was at this time that I had my first crush on a boy. His name was Johnny. What I liked about him was he wanted to protect us girls. If the boys were teasing us too much, he told them to stop. If I thought he was in a specific spot, I'd walk out of my way just to pass him and let him see me. If he saw me and wasn't preoccupied, he always said hello and gave me a big smile that melted my heart. Most of the times, when I was with my friend Joyce, I talked about Johnny. One time, Johnny offered to walk Joyce and me home. Joyce lived closer to where we hung out, so Johnny walked me further without her. I was beyond excited and so frightened of my feelings toward him. I had never felt those kinds of feelings before, and I blushed every time he looked at me. We were hanging out in front of my apartment building. I don't remember our conversation, but Johnny gave me his high school ring to hold. He told me I could wear it but to return it the next time I saw him. At the time, I assumed he realized I had a crush on him, and he was just being kind to me. That was why I had a crush on him. He was so nice to everyone. He had such a big heart. Always a perfect gentleman.

The next day, when it came time to do the dinner dishes, I took the ring off and put it on the washing machine next to the sink. I didn't want to damage it while doing the dishes. When I was ready to put the ring back on my finger, I couldn't find it. It was no longer where I left it. I looked for it for days. I even pulled out the washing machine and looked behind it, but I never found the ring. I avoided looking for Johnny for fear he would ask for his ring back, but he never did. I don't think it meant that much to him. I finally told him I lost it, and he said not to worry about it. I was so relieved. What a great person.

When I happened to see Johnny and he smiled at me, I spent hours at night with my friends trying to figure out what that meant. I loved singing songs that had Johnny's name in it, such as "Johnny Angel." One day, my friend Joyce had a picture of Johnny. She never told me how she got it. He must have given it to her. At the time, it didn't dawn on me that he must like her if he gave her his picture. I begged her to give the picture to me, and she did. I was in heaven. I spent hours daydreaming about him. Four years later, Joyce married Johnny.

My first part-time job was working as a receptionist in a shop that made signs. I enjoyed the work, but it didn't last long. The owner tried to come on to me several times, and I ignored it but then I decided it wasn't worth having to deal with his bad behavior and quit.

Attending Eli Whitney Vocational High School had many challenges. Certain boys in class were disruptive toward the teacher and bullied many of the girls, including me. My last name—Goldberg—was a problem for some of the other students.

There were two horrible and frightening experiences in school. The first one happened while I was waiting for an interview to try out for cheerleader. I felt terrified but thought, *Ruthie, take a risk. You have nothing to lose. Try out.* But while waiting for my turn, one of the girls also waiting started making fun of me. It bothered her that I was going for the interview. By the time I was called in for the interview, I was paralyzed with fear. After the interview was over, I found a group of girls outside the building waiting for me. One particular girl wanted to beat me up. I must have said something she didn't like while she was bullying me. She slapped me and pulled my hair. I ran to the corner police station and reported her and her friends. The police came up to school the next day and gave them a warning. After that day, they left me alone.

My sophomore year in high school, I had a painful experience in history class that changed my life forever. I always knew I was bright, and I promised myself never to quit school even though I was bullied by kids in my classes. For some reason, I was an easy target. I looked awkward and had a big nose and a Jewish last name. At times, I answered back to defend myself, and it made things worse. In history class that day, the teacher was teaching about Israel. A girl in the back of the class knew I had a Jewish last name and yelled out, "Hey, Goldberg, why don't you answer the question? You're a Jew."

I already had insecurities about being half-Jewish. I didn't need this comment. I told her to mind her own business. That was a big mistake. She came from the back of the room and pushed me, saying, "Make me."

A big fight started with other students, too, and the teacher was in the middle of it. When the fight was finally stopped, we were brought to the principal's office. The girl told the principal I called her names. I explained to the principal what actually happened. I was devastated. This whole experience affected me so much that I didn't want to go to school anymore. I couldn't take it any longer. I decided to quit school. The disrespect from other students affected my ability to learn. It was bad enough that I had problems at home. I hated that I never felt safe in school, but I couldn't believe I was quitting. This was the one time my mother came up to school. She had to sign me out.

A few weeks later, I received a $500 check in the mail as a result of being hit by a car sometime earlier. I decided to use the money to attend a private secretarial school. I went for the interview and was accepted. But little did I know, the classroom was in the basement of the house of the woman who ran the school. The teacher had vintage 1920 typewriters with thick black letters. I stayed in the school for a few months but found out the teacher's methods didn't help me to be successful. We had to do most of the work on our own. I needed more individual instruction than I was getting. When the semester was over, I did not return. At this time, I was unhappy at home and had to figure out what to do with my life.

These were my teenage years, and at times they were difficult. I learned early on that it was up to me to make my life work. I also realized that the choices I made would affect my life in the future. I was an independent girl with a deep faith in God. I knew that the mistakes I made helped me become stronger and gave me strength to never give up.

Chapter 9

Both my mother and stepfather, Jimmy, were heavy smokers. Mom was extremely nervous. She smoked about four packs of cigarettes a day. Often, she sent me to the store for them. I went to a store where the cigarettes were a few cents cheaper, so I could buy myself a piece of candy with the leftover money. As long as Mother received her cigarettes, she was happy.

As I said before, Jimmy worked in a rag company filled with dust particles.

I came home from school one day and was told Mother had gone to Connecticut to get married to Jimmy. They were living common law for years, but they had decided to get married. I found out later that Jimmy got married to protect my mother and his two girls, Connie and Maryann, because he had lung cancer. I had no idea about cancer. I was naive about serious illnesses.

The Death of My Stepfather, Jimmy Babino

Not long after Mom and Jimmy were married, Jimmy had to go to the hospital because of his lung cancer. I thought for sure he would come home, but instead, in 1965, he passed away. I was sorry to hear the news. I always liked Jimmy. Even though he was an alcoholic, he was a good man. When he wasn't drunk, he was fun to be around. He treated me fairly. I felt safe in some way having him home. But another part of me was relieved that the fighting with him and my mother was now over.

When Jimmy died, I was fifteen years old. I knew my mother was sad, but she didn't share it or show it. I thought there would be more peace in our home. But she grieved by getting drunk more often, especially on the weekends. She liked to drink, felt lonely, and liked being around other people her age. One night, while I was watching out the window, one of the neighbors called to me from the street and said, "Ruthie, you need to go get your mother out of the bar." The bar was across the street from our apartment.

"Your mother is drunk and acting it," the neighbor said.

I got dressed and went to the bar and brought Mother home. I could hardly hold her up. She was drunk and acting silly.

This incident irritated me. There were other similar ones throughout those times. I felt embarrassed that the neighbors had to see my mother drunk.

A few months after Jimmy died, I was hanging out with my girlfriend. We were on a corner near St. Francis of Paola Church, sitting and talking about parents. My friend said something mean about my mother, and I was defending her. As I finished talking, I happened to turn around. My mother was drunk on the opposite corner near the bar. It was broad daylight, and she was making out with some old man right in front of everyone. I almost died. I wanted to crawl in a hole. My hands and knees trembled. I couldn't believe she would have such bad behavior in broad daylight. I decided my mother was lonely and out of control with her feelings.

I remember a few times when my stepfather's mother, Mary, treated me kindly and generously. Sometimes she took me shopping for an outfit and a new pair of pajamas. Then we went home to her apartment, and she made dinner. I loved being at her home. I slept in my new pajamas in such a peaceful environment. After Jimmy died, I never knew what happened to Mary. I never saw her again.

One joyful time was my sister Annie's wedding day. She looked radiant. I was a bridesmaid and had a beautiful silk, royal blue dress with a matching bow in my hair. It was an honor to stand up for Annie. She had a kind and caring personality. She would give me the shirt off her back if I asked for it. My love for Annie went deep. We shared so much pain and joy together. Annie's wedding day was the first time I experienced so many family members celebrating together. It was so wonderful being with my aunts, uncles, cousins, and grandparents.

When I was alone, I found tears running down my face every time I thought of Annie not living with us anymore.

My mother used profanity constantly, especially when she felt I was moving too slowly to suit her. I wasn't happy living home, but I had nowhere else to go. I remember thinking, *I wished I lived in a peaceful environment and had my own room.* But I had no idea how that could ever happen.

Leaving Greenpoint, Brooklyn

One time I had a fight with my younger sister Maryann. I wish it had never happened, but it did. I don't remember what the fight was about. But I do remember my mother blaming me. She was not only emotionally abusive but physically abusive as well. She beat me and pounded on my back with all her anger. She had done that to me in the past too. I didn't want to live with her anymore. After feeling hurt and sad, I called my father. I expressed how wounded I felt after mother beat me up. I announced that I did not want to live with her anymore. I asked him if he had any suggestions. A short time later, my father called and asked me if I wanted to live with Aunt Jessie, Uncle Hyme, and my three cousins.

I said, "Daddy, if I live with Aunt Jessie, I would like her to enroll me into a high school near her." He said she would.

I was sorry that I hurt my mother by moving out, but I needed a more stable environment. I was confused. I knew it would have been an intolerable situation for me to continue living at home. I had just begun a relationship with my first boyfriend, and I didn't want my home life to get in the way.

My faith in God became the only thing I could hold onto in a moment of total despair. All I had to do was believe it would all work out, and I was thrilled about going back to high school. I felt in my heart this change was God's will for me.

Chapter 10

My relationship with my mother caused me emotional pain. I rarely saw my father. My sister Annie was married and out of the apartment. My sister June worked and stayed with her friends most of the time.

Meeting My First Boyfriend

I met Bobby two months before my sixteenth birthday. He stuck with me through all the chaos and upset taking place in my life at school and at home. He stayed by my side when I moved to Aunt Jessie's apartment. He was my boyfriend, and I knew he cared. I did not have good role models in my life, but I had Bobby and his family.

I met Bobby when my girlfriend and her sister mentioned that they were going to a party at a social club in the Bedford Stuyvesant section of Brooklyn, New York, and they invited me to come along. I thought as long as we were together, it would be safe. The neighborhood itself was mixed, but the social club was in an area where mostly Italians lived. We enjoyed going to the club on weekends whenever we could. We had fun listening to music, playing pool, Ping-Pong, or dancing. Everyone was open and friendly. The men looked out for the safety of the ladies.

In the beginning, Bobby and his friends did not come to the club. We met them in the candy store around the corner. When we arrived in the area, my friend and I took walks around their block so that they would notice us. When we knew they were in the candy store, we went for a soda. We both thought the boys were good-looking, and we were interested in getting to know them. As time went on, the boys began showing up at the social club looking for us.

When I first met Bobby, he wanted me to go with his cousin Anthony, but I wasn't interested. I was interested in him. Eventually, Bobby realized I had a crush on him, and we started to like each other. I thought he was good-looking, and I found him extremely attractive. He was smart, made me laugh, and was attentive when I spoke. I felt comfortable around him. He was a gentleman and showed self-confidence. I was overly excited spending time with Bobby. He was my first boyfriend.

Bobby's close friend was interested in my friend. When it was time for us to go home to Greenpoint, both boys walked us to the bus stop. The first time Bobby kissed me, I was thrilled! I couldn't stop thinking about that kiss. Shortly after the kiss, he asked me, "Ruthie, do you want to go out with me?"

Of course, I said, "Yes."

In the beginning of my relationship with Bobby, my girlfriend and I still hung out in his neighborhood. Many times, we went to Bobby's friend's finished basement and listened to music, Beatles music a lot of the time. The *Rubber Soul* album was one of my favorites. We all sang along to the songs and had lots of laughs together.

The boys were heavily into sports, so when a game was on television, we all watched it together. Sports was never my thing, but just being with Bobby was what I enjoyed.

Shortly after Bobby and I started dating, I found out that he went to church on Sunday and was a freshman in college at St. John's University. He was the oldest child in his family, with three sisters and a baby brother. Bobby also told me his father allowed him to use his car. When I got home after our date that night, I realized Bobby was the boy I had prayed for every day for two years. I was astounded and filled with joy. The Lord had heard my prayers and answered them.

None of Bobby's childhood friends were in college. Most of

them were seniors in high school. Bobby had skipped a grade and graduated before his friends. His cousin Anthony worked full-time.

One night while hanging out with Bobby, we were taking a walk, and he made a comment that affected me. He said, "There are two kinds of people in the world, Italians and people who wished they were Italian." He then said, "There is only one thing worse than not being Italian, and that is to be Jewish."

I thought, *Here we go again with the Jewish thing.*

I almost died. Up to this point, he had not asked me my last name. But when he told his mother about me, she asked him my last name, and he said he did not know. She said, "You mean you don't know her last name? Ask her!"

So, he did.

I told him my name was Graziano, which is my mother's maiden name. I was too afraid to tell him the truth, for fear he would break up with me.

Bobby and I spent a lot of time together, especially on the weekends. Also, we had so much fun double dating with his friends and their girlfriends. Eventually, Bobby started coming to my neighborhood. He met my mother and my sisters.

Ruthie, Mother, and Annie

On weekends, he often came to my neighborhood to pick me up, and we got together with his friends from college.

On Sunday, Bobby picked me up with his father's car. We went to Mass together and went to his house for dinner. I'd grown to like dinner with Bobby's family. I felt accepted. I thought highly of his mother, Nora. She was outspoken and gave her opinion openly and honestly at any time. I often helped Bobby's sisters, Diane and Denise or Linda, set the table or later do the dishes. It was an opportunity to get to know them better. And I enjoyed being around them.

After dinner, Bobby drove me home. He couldn't hang out at my apartment because there was no privacy.

One day six months after we began dating, I told Bobby I had something to tell him but that I was uncomfortable sharing it. I didn't want him to be upset with me.

He said, "Ruthie, you could tell me anything. I promise I will be understanding."

I told Bobby that I had lied about my last name because of the comment he had made, and I reminded him what he said. He told me he didn't remember saying it.

He said, "Ruthie, I care about you. Your last name doesn't matter to me."

I was happy with his reaction.

When I first started dating Bobby, we spent time cuddling and kissing whenever we could. Those experiences were always so thrilling. We both chose not to go further. We were both good Catholics and believed that any further would lead to more. Since Bobby was my first boyfriend, it brought new challenges into my life. Every intimate step we took was new for me. There were times I spent hours the next day just thinking about the kiss and how exciting it felt.

Around this time, Bobby was not doing well at St. John's, and his mother and father went up to the academic adviser to discuss his options. He was put on probation, and his parents told him if he didn't pick up his grades, he would not be allowed to see me anymore or use their car. I couldn't believe my ears when Bobby first told me the news. He promised he would apply himself, and he did. He raised his grades, and we continued to see each other.

Chapter 11

The day I left my mother's apartment was bittersweet. I had a sense of loss in my heart, especially knowing I would not see my little sisters. I felt grief wondering if Maryann thought I was leaving because of our fight. I hugged her and said, "Maryann, I love you and promise I will keep in touch." And I did.

My heart was pounding. I felt totally drained both physically and emotionally. I wondered whether or not my mother wanted me to leave, even though she hadn't said anything. Sometimes I didn't think she loved me at all. I loved her and gave my best, which was never enough. If I wanted a relationship with her, I realized I had to be the one to reach out, and at this time, I was not ready. But I was ready to experience a new chapter in my life.

My father came to take me to Aunt Jessie's. I gave my mother a hug and said, "I am sorry I hurt you, but me moving in with Aunt Jessie is for the better right now."

She said, "I want what is best for you."

I said, "I love you, Mommy, and I will keep in touch."

Living with Aunt Jessie, Uncle Hyme, and My Three Cousins

At Aunt Jessie's, my cousin Warren agreed to give me his room and sleep on a cot in the living room for two years.

Aunt Jessie and Warren

Aunt Jessie said, "Ruthie, I promise you can stay with us until you graduate from high school, and then we will see."

For the first time in my life, I had my own room, and I was so happy. Warren emptied out a dresser for me to use. The room was bright and spacious, with two big windows and pretty light blue curtains with a matching bedspread. I thought, *This is another dream come true.*

Aunt Jessie's apartment was spotless. You could eat off the floor, and I was now living in a stable environment. They lived in a housing project on the Lower East Side of New York City. Actually, it was my first time in Manhattan. Uncle Hyme was in charge of the security for the building. He ran a community center on the ground floor, which kept many of the kids who lived in the building off the streets. This was a lower-income neighborhood. I had to have eyes in the back of my head when I was outside. At this time, I was seventeen. I wasn't afraid because usually I only went outside at night with Bobby or, later on, with my friend Sarah.

Bobby and I always had fun together. One Easter Sunday in 1967, I looked cute and elegant, and Bobby looked so handsome. We attended Mass and had a special breakfast of pancakes and sausage. We took the car and went to Prospect Park to walk around. We had a good time laughing and joking. We had a wonderful Easter day together.

Bobby loved the Yankees, and we loved going to their games. One time, we took Bobby's little brother along, and as the pitch went out and the ball was hit, it flew directly into my hands. What a miracle and so thrilling. I gave the ball to his little brother. I knew it would mean a lot to him.

Many times, Bobby invited me to activities at St. John's University. He belonged to a fraternity, Beta Sigma Roe. Bobby enjoyed being part of a group of men who enjoyed college. In my opinion, they were all good men.

We went to St. John's basketball games and campus parties and saw several great concerts: Peter, Paul, and Mary; Frankie Valli and the Four Seasons; Chicago; and many others. I love music, and I enjoyed all the fun activities we participated in at St. John's.

Most of the girlfriends of Bobby's friends were students at St. John's studying to be teachers. One time I remember thinking, *How lucky these girls are to have good parents and attend a great school, studying to be teachers. If only I had different parents, I would go to St. John's University.*

I had an internal struggle. Although I felt sexy and good about myself being Bobby's girlfriend, I felt that I didn't fit in with the girlfriends of his friends. I had nothing in common with them. They were more educated than me and came from upper-middle class families. Their parents were paying for their education. They never gave me a reason to feel that way, but it was my own insecurities.

A Meaningful Visit with the Homecoming Queen

One day, there was a festival that was part of the St. John's football team celebration. I was shocked to see the homecoming queen. She was one of my friends from the orphanage. Her name was Maggie. It gave me a sense of pride seeing her as homecoming queen. We hugged, and I let her know how happy I was to see her so successful. She agreed she was doing well. We really couldn't talk much because she was on a platform. My one regret is that I didn't get her contact information.

With all the turmoil taking place in my personal life, I have to say I was blessed the day I met Bobby. We both had a lot of growing up to do, but I believed we would grow together.

Returning to High School

The first week I lived with Aunt Jessie, she took me to register and return to school. I attended Seward Park High School. I was thrilled to be back. I never wanted to quit high school. I thought, *This is truly a second chance.*

Being at Seward Park High School was such a great experience. Everyone was respectful and friendly. No one yelled out in class, and I enjoyed school. I even made the honor roll several times. I had to make up the six months of school that I missed, and my intention was to graduate in January 1968.

My First Real Part-Time Job

Now that I was settled in with Aunt Jessie and attending school, I knew I had to find a part-time job. I went to an employment agency, and I was sent immediately on an interview and was hired right away. My job was in an office at Retail Jenny Shop's. I entered all the receipts for merchandise and balanced the books on the adding machine. I also was a receptionist and answered the phones. I enjoyed being independent and having my own money. I also was able to get my cousin Arthur a job in the shipping department. It was great seeing him at work.

After work, I went right home, had dinner, did the dishes, then did my homework. I mostly stayed in my room at night, except when Bobby called, since the phone was in the kitchen. He called most nights since I only saw him on weekends or when we had a day off from school. At this time, Bobby was a junior in college, worked part-time, and had his own car.

While in high school, I met Sarah. She became a good friend. We spent a lot of time together. She lived a few buildings down from Aunt Jessie's building and was the only friend I had at school. I usually saw Sarah on Friday nights because it was rare that I saw Bobby.

In my junior year of high school, I wanted to try to learn Pitman stenography. I tried to learn it in the secretarial school I previously attended for a short time but wasn't successful. I took Steno 1 and 2 in my first two semesters and received a 95 percent average. Since I did so well, I registered for summer school to complete Steno 3 and 4, since I planned on graduating in January. I was never told it was not a good idea to take transcription in a summer class. I spent much of the summer struggling. It was nothing like I expected. The teacher told me that many of the students failed, and they were reviewing the class. She thought I should not feel so bad. I decided it was a lesson learned. I didn't need this course to graduate, so I didn't complete it.

While living at Aunt Jessie's, I usually saw Bobby on Saturday night and sometimes on Sunday during the day. Some Sundays, Bobby and I went to St. Teresa's Church across the street, then to his family's home to hang out and for dinner.

Aunt Jessie and Uncle Hyme and my cousins were of the Jewish faith. But Aunt Jessie always encouraged me to go to church. I appreciated her support. For me, she represented the mother I never had. She was always caring and showed her concern. She often asked me how school was going and at times asked if I got my homework done, especially on a Sunday night when I wanted to go out somewhere.

I rarely saw my mother while living in Manhattan, except on certain holidays, Thanksgiving, Christmas, Easter, or her birthday. Bobby often came with me to visit her. I called her every week to see how she was feeling. I loved my mother just because she was my mother. I wished that she was competent enough to reach out to me. As time went on, I realized that she was not capable of it. Because of this, I appreciated Aunt Jessie even more. She was giving me some of what I longed for from my mother.

One time, several days went by without a call from Bobby. It was unlike him. I couldn't understand what had happened. When he did call, he just told me he would see me Saturday afternoon and that he couldn't talk. He didn't sound right on the phone.

Saturday came, and I was a nervous wreck. When Bobby arrived, he told me that he was breaking up with me. I was devastated and blindsided. He said he needed time. We had been going out for about two years.

I cried for days. For a whole day after he left, I cried. I felt that my whole world was ending. He was the one stable person I thought cared about me. I couldn't believe he didn't want me in his life anymore. For a whole week, I walked around in a daze of disbelief.

After a week, Bobby called to see how I was doing.

"Bobby, I miss you very much," I said.

He said, "I am sorry for hurting you. I didn't want to hurt you."

Very shortly after that phone call, Bobby called again and said, "Ruthie, can I come and see you?"

When Bobby came to pick me up, I was filled with joy. We had a good time. We went to the South Street Seaport and walked along holding hands. He kept hugging me. Later we went for a delicious shrimp dinner. I remember thinking, *How could he not want me in his life when I love him so much?*

After our date, Bobby took me home and told me he wanted me back and that he had made a mistake and he missed me a lot.

I was on cloud nine. It felt so right being together again.

We used to hang out in my room. Aunt Jessie let us. We both lived by Christian values. We kissed a lot, and when it got too heated, we stopped. I loved the closeness.

In May of Bobby's Junior year at college, he invited me to his junior prom. I bought a beautiful, long, pale pink dress with an attractive Victorian collar with white lace. My hair at the time was blond, and I had it styled, and it looked terrific. I felt sexy and beautiful.

The prom was at an exclusive club on Long Island. We had a table with all Bobby's friends and their girlfriends. It was a wonderful evening. We laughed, ate delicious food, and danced the night away.

When he drove me home that night, we were the most intimate ever, and it frightened me. But that night, I couldn't stop thinking about how close I felt.

Living with Aunt Jessie, Uncle Hyme, Warren, Robert, and Arthur were wonderful. I felt peaceful and loved having my own room. My father came to visit a couple of times a month, and I cherished seeing him. He gave Aunt Jessie a little bit of money for food to help with me.

I very rarely spent time with my cousins. They had their own lives and were out a lot. I did see Arthur at work since we worked for the same company. It was a good feeling seeing him daily.

Aunt Jessie was a great cook, and she was always cleaning the apartment. When she wanted me to clean my room, she let me know, and I cleaned it. She wanted everything to be spotless. She understood I had a busy schedule with school and work and was considerate of my time.

My regular chore was to do the dishes. It is funny, even today I do not mind doing the dishes, since it was my job often in my younger years.

Since working for over a year part-time, making eighty-five cents an hour, I decided I deserved a raise. I found out the new person who was just hired made more money than I did. I went to my boss and asked for a fifteen-cent raise. He said he couldn't afford it. I worked hard the few hours a day I was in the office. I felt let down, so I gave my two-week notice and quit. It was difficult facing my boss for the two weeks. I agreed to work since I am a woman of integrity.

The last day of work, I stood in the hallway waiting for the elevator to leave the building for the last time. I had tears streaming down my face. I couldn't believe they didn't think I was worth a raise when I was responsible, reliable, and always did a good job.

At the time, there were employment agencies everywhere wanting to find jobs for people. I went to an agency, confident that I was a good deal and worth hiring. One week later, I obtained a new job working for an insurance broker, typing up invoices and binders and delivering them to the insurance companies for signatures. I started at a dollar twenty an hour. It was a thirty-five-cent raise from my last job. I was proud that I knew I was worth more and stood my ground and quit the other job. I enjoyed going out into the field to get signatures. I met interesting people along the way.

As I continued to work, I saved a little of my money each week and eventually bought my own portable Zenith television. It was my first big purchase, and Bobby and I both enjoyed watching television together.

In my senior year of high school, I decided to fill out an application for college. I was elated with the thought that I would be going to college. I applied to Baruch College on Twenty-Third Street, New York City. Baruch is a business college. Bobby was a big influence on me, and I wanted to make him and his family proud.

One day, I received a letter from the education department, and I almost died. The letter informed me that I hadn't been accepted. The college admissions suggested I first attend a place for remedial work that I needed, so I could be accepted upon completion of those courses. I took this as a big rejection and decided I would be going straight to work. Little did I know that after graduation, I would need to find somewhere else to live. I could not have attended college full-time anyway.

My High School Graduation

Graduation day was wonderful. Bobby, my father, Aunt Jessie, and Uncle Hyme attended. I thought, *This day finally came. I am so proud of myself that I made it.*

Uncle Hyme, Ruthie, and Daddy—high school graduation day

I wore a dark blue cap and gown. I had bought my dress myself—a lime green, fitted dress with a V-neck collar. It looked very sexy on me. I had blond hair at the time. I had my hair done in the neighborhood beauty parlor the day before.

None of my sisters or my mother attended my graduation, but my mother sent me one hundred dollars. It was her way of letting me know she was proud of me. She did call me when we returned home for a small celebration at my aunt's apartment. She told me she was proud of me and happy that I was successful. I believed she meant it.

I assumed my older sisters were working, but I didn't know for sure. My little sisters were in school, and no one could take them from Brooklyn to Manhattan.

Bobby bought me a 14-carat gold ankle bracelet with two hearts interlocking and a diamond chip in the middle with our names engraved. I loved it.

Shortly after graduation day, Aunt Jessie told me I needed to find somewhere else to live. She agreed to give me a few weeks to find a place. I now had to find a full-time job and then find a place to live. I was shocked. I actually didn't think this would happen so soon, but my cousin needed his room back.

Warren giving me his room so that I could finish high school was the most generous gift anyone could have given me. Every time I see my cousin Warren, I remind him how much it meant to me that he gave me his room. Even today I remind him. For him, it was no big deal; he didn't mind. But to me, it was a very big deal. I love my cousin and always will remember his generosity.

I could not imagine going back to live with my mother. There was no way I could tolerate that life again. I didn't know what to do. I appreciated Aunt Jessie being there for me for two years. She gave me the best two years of my life and provided peace and tranquility. I did well in school and had the space to study. She cooked and cleaned the apartment and rarely asked me to help her clean. She showed her love by her actions. I will never forget her kindness. I have nothing but love for Aunt Jessie, Uncle Hyme, and my cousins. Aunt Jessie was the mother I longed for, and she provided exactly what I needed. I felt truly grateful for all she did for me during those two years. My graduating high school was another dream come true.

Back to the Employment Agency

I knew I had to find a full-time job, so I decided to go to an employment agency. It was amazing how fast I found a job at Courts & Company, a brokerage firm with its main office in Atlanta, Georgia. The job was on Wall Street. I obtained the job because of my typing skills. I worked in the cage, taking in stocks and bonds, and typing up the forms for intake. At first, I trembled because I could not make a mistake with the form or I had to cancel the form number. But I became good at the job as I built up my confidence.

Next, I had to find a place to live. It was coming close to the two-week mark. Aunt Jessie let me know that if I needed another week or so, it was fine. I have to admit, whenever I thought about my next move, I began shaking like a leaf. Fear of the unknown clouded my mind, especially since I could not predict the outcome. All I could do was pray that the Holy Spirit would lead me in the direction I needed to go.

On Sunday, I went to St. Teresa's for church. After Mass, I asked the priest if I could speak with him. I explained my situation. I asked if he could help me find a place to live. I explained why I couldn't return to my mother's apartment. I had to make it on my own.

He gave me a phone number to call. Later on, I understood I was calling Catholic Charities of New York. They gave me an appointment for an interview.

The day of the interview, I prayed that Catholic Charities could find me a place to live. I couldn't bear the thought of having no choice but to move back home with my mother. I had become a more peaceful person, and I wanted to stay that way.

I was apprehensive when I arrived for the interview. An amiable lady asked me a million questions. After I answered the questions successfully, she made some phone calls. She then told me I had an interview with Queen of Peace in Brooklyn, New York, on Eighth Street and Prospect Park Avenue. This facility was run by Catholic sisters. The residence was for young women who were employed but had no place to live.

The day of the interview, I explained to my supervisor at work that I had to find a place to live, and she gave me the day off. I felt anxious going to the interview.

When I arrived at Queen of Peace, I had butterflies in my stomach. I rang the bell, and Sister Elizabeth opened the door. She had a big smile that made me a little more comfortable. During the interview, Sister explained that all the girls shared rooms and that two meals a day, breakfast and dinner, were provided. She also said there was a curfew of 11:00 p.m. on weekdays and 1:00 a.m. on weekends. The rent was affordable, since I worked and made good money. Sister explained if a girl didn't make curfew, she needed to sleep somewhere else. Sister agreed to take me in and showed me my room. I left feeling excitement and joy knowing I had a place to live. We settled on my day of arrival, and I thanked her for the opportunity.

Life became another new adventure. I hoped to meet new friends and to have the strength to start all over again. I believed I did. I had control over my life, and I chose to make it work, no matter what it took.

I also knew that because of my faith in God, his providence led me to what was next for me. I felt safe, knowing the sisters were managing the residence. This was something I was familiar with, and I knew it was divine providence leading the way.

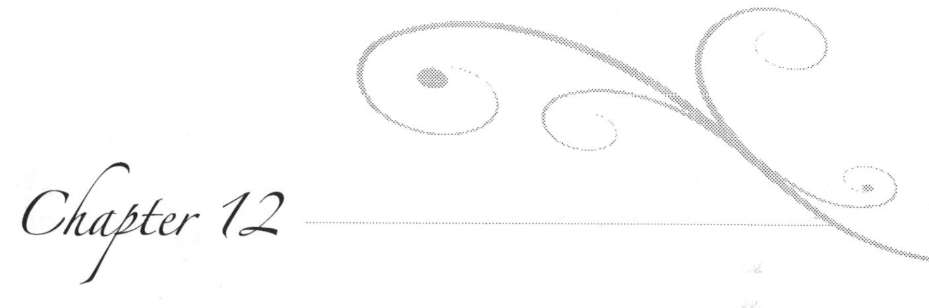

Chapter 12

The day I moved in was unnerving. I didn't know what to expect.

The room I first moved into had four girls. Anne and I had the back of the room. We had three windows and an unusable fireplace with a mantelpiece. I loved placing my pictures on the mantel. Our room was separated by sliding white wooden doors. We closed the doors if we were resting or sleeping or on the phone.

Anne explained that her mother was deceased. Anne had been living with her father, but it wasn't working out. She was a warm, kind woman. I thought she was a perfect roommate.

Anne gave me permission to receive phone calls on her phone, and I appreciated it. I let her know it would only be my boyfriend, Bobby, or my mother calling. She was fine with me sharing her phone. She said her father paid her bill.

There was a phone in the main hallway, and when one of us had a call, the girl who answered the phone notified us. It was so much better for Bobby to call on a private line in my room. We spoke on the phone most nights, even if sometimes it was just to say good night. Anne was a blessing to live with. She was kind, quiet, and open. I enjoyed our new friendship. I also enjoyed sharing my television with her, and we both enjoyed watching it together.

The experience of living with a house full of girls reminded me of a college dorm. Although I had never experienced college dorms, I had seen them in movies.

A dinner bell rang when it was time for dinner. If we wanted to eat, we filed into the dining room.

As a full-time employee, I decided to obtain my first charge card at G&G shops. Whenever I wanted a new outfit, I went shopping, whether or not I had the money. If they didn't have anything nice in my size, I was out of luck. But when they did have the perfect outfit for me, it brought joy to my heart. I had been financially responsible since I began working. I was never willing to be in debt. Even today, I pay every bill on time and never pay a finance charge.

Life was peaceful during this time in my life. I enjoyed my job at Courts & Company. Bobby landed a part-time job in the same building as me on a different floor. Often, we met on one of the floors we didn't work on and spent a few minutes kissing hello. We were both passionate about each other. We met after work and took the subway home together toward Brooklyn, New York.

Another Breakup with Bobby

Once, going home on the subway, Bobby asked me to hold his jacket. While I was holding it, an envelope fell out of his pocket. I picked it up and noticed it was from another girl. I couldn't believe it. I was angry and hurt and broke up with him. I didn't know what else to do. I was disappointed, sad, and tearful all at once. I had been so sure we were doing well together.

Bobby confessed that when he went upstate with some of his friends for a weekend, he had met a girl. He admitted they were writing to each other. I cried for several days and did not take his calls.

When I look back now, I realize how young we were. I was eighteen, and he was nineteen. I was his first girlfriend, and it was normal for him to want to date others and compare what he had with me. I probably should have also dated other men to compare, but I was so much in love.

After a week of not taking his calls, I received a dozen red roses with a note saying how sorry he felt and how he didn't want to lose me. I felt his love, and I totally forgave him. I loved Bobby. He meant everything to me, and I didn't want to lose him to another woman.

Usually when we went out, it was with other couples or to Bobby's families for dinner. Very rarely did we go out alone. Because Bobby wanted to show me what I meant to him, he took me to a unique restaurant. The restaurant was made up of private cars that were part of a train. I enjoyed greatly the entire experience. The food was excellent. Being together was fun and romantic, and I felt loved.

It was time for Bobby's graduation festivities. He invited me to his senior prom. I bought a beautiful light-colored dress made of sequins of white and beige. It had a V-neck collar, and it looked beautiful and sexy on me. Bobby loved it. He complimented me all night long. The prom was held at Terrace on the Park, Queens, New York. We had a table with all our friends and had a great time laughing, dancing, eating, and drinking. The food was delicious. We always had fun when we were together with Bobby's college friends, and this was a special evening.

The Big Day

Bobby's graduation day from St. John's University was outside. It was a bright, sunny day. There was not one cloud in the sky. Bobby's whole family was present as well as his friends and their girlfriends. Most of them were in the same year and also graduated. I looked great, with a light blue dress, and my hair was brown again and was up in curls on top and long at the back. I always dressed to please Bobby, and he was pleased. After graduation, there were pictures, and the whole family went to an Italian restaurant to celebrate. It was a great day. I wished I was a student at St. John's University. It was my dream.

At one point while living at Queen of Peace, Anne asked me if I wanted to move into another room with just the two of us. I agreed, believing it would be much less noise during the night when we wanted to sleep. While I enjoyed my room, usually I couldn't fall asleep until the two girls in the front room went to bed. They were usually up until midnight or later. Both Anne and I liked to be in bed by 11:00 p.m. It didn't work for us that they were up when we wanted to sleep. Ann notified Sister that we were requesting a room change when one became available. When a room on the other side of the building became available, we agreed to take it. At the beginning, it was great for the most part. The girls in the rooms next to us were in and out of their rooms and often loud in the hallway, but they always quieted down by 10:00 p.m., and that was good for us. Many times, Anne didn't come home on the weekends. I believe she stayed at her father's house.

Changing My Nose

While living at Queen of Peace, I thought about getting a nose job. Ever since I could remember, people had told me I looked like Barbara Streisand. I had her nose and facial structure. I knew my nose was big, and I had hated being picked on in the past because of it. Bobby told me a nose job was my decision. He didn't want me to blame him if it didn't come out right. I decided to do it. I found a plastic surgeon at Grand Army Plaza, Brooklyn, New York. Dr. Miceli examined me and informed me that I had a deviated septum and he was willing to fix the problem. He agreed to charge my father's insurance. I appreciated his willingness to work with me. The day I went for the surgery, every bone in my body shook. I hated being around hospitals. I was told they couldn't put me to sleep because I needed to be able to breathe. The doctor gave me something for the pain, and he began to work. I heard them banging on my nose and making comments. I didn't feel anything. I lay there praying that I would be safe.

The day after surgery, I was released from the hospital and had to return to the doctor's office in 3 days to get the bandages off. I set it up with my mother to stay at her apartment. She was supportive and happy to help. It was also an opportunity to see my two little sisters, Maryann and Connie. I didn't have much time to spend with them since they were in school those days. Also, Mother was at work during the day. I took vacation time off from work, and good thing I did.

The day I had to return to the doctor's office, I prayed that my nose didn't look terrible. When I arrived, the doctor was ready to take off the bandages. I was petrified that I wouldn't like my new nose. I was also concerned that Bobby would not like it. When I looked in the mirror, I was horrified at how turned up it was. I looked like an Irish pelican. The doctor told me to give it time, that it was swollen. I didn't believe him and left his office in tears.

A day or two later, while I was back home, I started to bleed. My nose would not stop bleeding. After contacting the doctor, I was advised to return to the hospital. I had to have my nose cauterized and packed, and then I was sent home again. My mother was concerned when she saw the bleeding.

When I returned to get the packing out of my nose, I continued to bleed, so I had to stay in the hospital for another week. The doctor didn't understand why I kept bleeding. Later in life, I discovered I had a mild platelet problem, and whenever I have surgery, I have to inform my doctors.

Bobby stayed by my side the entire time. He visited me often. He was the only visitor I had. After a week, I finally stopped bleeding. The doctor said, "Ruth, you can go home after there has been no bleeding for twenty-four hours."

Finally, the swelling went down, and I started to like the way it looked, and so did Bobby. I actually considered myself very cute and sexy.

Having to Find a New Job Again

When I was nineteen, Courts & Company informed its employees that they were moving their New York office back to their home office in Atlanta, Georgia. It was a difficult time for me. I had to keep working to pay my rent. On the final day at Courts & Company, we had a goodbye luncheon. It was a sad day, saying goodbye to everyone I had worked with since January 1968. I had several friends I enjoyed seeing every day, especially Maureen. We agreed to stay in touch. But saying goodbye to others was disheartening. I knew I would never see them again.

The day ended early. We were told we could leave after the luncheon. I started walking down the street and got to the corner curb. I looked up, and Mr. Evans, the man who had gotten me the job at Courts & Company, was standing next to me. When he noticed me, he said hello and asked me how I was doing. I explained, "Mr. Evans, the job you obtained for me over a year and a half ago ended today."

He said, "Come by my office tomorrow, and I will get you another job."

I was astonished. I thought, *This is another miracle.* At that moment, I realized the Lord watches out for me and provides.

The next day, I went back to the agency to meet with Mr. Evans. I sat in his office for several hours, hoping he would find an interview. After the few hours, he called me into his office and explained he was sending me to Bankers Trust Company for an interview. I was thrilled yet scared. The interview was at the human resources office in the Wall Street area.

I walked into the office, and there were at least twenty other men and woman waiting for an interview. I thought, *How am I ever going to get a job at this office with so many people before me?*

I waited for over an hour and then decided to call the agency. I told Mr. Evans my predicament, and he said, "Ruthie, stay for the interview no matter how long it takes. They are very selective of who they hire, and you have a shot."

I agreed to stay. I had to trust him since I had nothing to lose.

About a half hour later, my name was called, and I was escorted into a typing pool to take a test. The process felt like an assembly line. I was escorted directly into the typing pool without anyone introducing themselves.

The instructor said, "Take a seat, and you will begin to take your test. When I say start, begin typing, and when I say stop, you stop typing." Those were the only instructions she gave.

When the instructor said start, I was incredibly nervous and noticed myself making numerous mistakes. One of the pupils taking the test kept asking questions while we were typing. I could not concentrate. At one point, the instructor said, "Stop typing. Take your paper out. We are going to begin the test again since I had interruptions with questions." She looked at all of us. "Does anyone else have a question?"

There was no response.

I was so appreciative that she gave us a second chance. We took the typing test again, and I did not make one mistake.

As I said earlier, I attribute my success as an excellent typist to my mother, since, years before, she had bought me the one gift that meant the world to me—a Royal portable typewriter.

I went back into the pool of people, and less than ten minutes later, I was called for an interview. The lady was wonderful. She said, "Ruth, I congratulate you for receiving a perfect score on your typing test. Would you be willing to be a Dictaphone secretary in our uptown office?"

By the time the interview was complete, it was late in the afternoon. The interviewer made an appointment for me to meet the men I would be working for at nine o'clock the next morning at the executive branch of Bankers Trust Company in the real estate department located at 280 Park Avenue, New York City.

This was my first time going uptown. I had to control myself from the nervousness I felt in my body. I was given the directions to get to the job. Once I have directions, it is easier for me to find where I am going. When I reached my stop, I said a prayer that the Lord would guide me through the interview, and I would get the job.

When I came up out of the subway station to the street, I couldn't believe how beautiful uptown looked. There were flowerbeds with beautiful flowers all along the middle of the streets that defined the uptown and downtown traffic. I was amazed how clean and manicured the area looked. I went into this fancy building, up an escalator to the elevator bank, and then to the twentieth floor.

I entered the real estate department and informed the receptionist that I was there to see Mr. Dreyer and Mr. Byrnes. They were two vice presidents who were much older men. I would be working directly for them. She announced my name, and Mr. Byrnes came out to welcome me and escort me into their conference room.

The conference room was massive. It had a huge, wooden, shiny table and leather chairs all around the table. Mr. Dreyer invited me to sit at the table. Then both Mr. Dreyer and Mr. Byrnes began asking me a lot of personal questions. I told them I lived at Queen of Peace, a residence for working girls in Brooklyn. I answered each question as honestly as I could. I let them know that I had no experience using a Dictaphone. They agreed I should have no problem, and they hired me on the spot. I realized later I was already hired by human resources. The interview by my two new bosses was to get to know me. I believe they liked my personality. I was sweet and conscientious. I was to begin my job on Monday at 9:00 a.m.

First Day at Bankers Trust Company

Monday morning, I arrived at 9:00 sharp to start my new job. I felt excited and fearful all at the same time. Fear of the unknown yet excited that I was given this opportunity to work for two vice presidents. This was an accomplishment from typing forms all day at my last job, and I wanted to do a good job.

I was told to report to human resources to fill out several forms.

My starting pay would be $125 a week. I felt excited and proud of myself. It was a raise from my last job. When the forms were completed, I reported to the real estate department.

I felt comfortable commuting to the Upper East Side daily, and it worked out perfectly. Learning the Dictaphone seemed difficult. I was in the dictionary every minute. In those Days, we did not have spell-check. It was a good thing there was no time limit for my work to get done. Mr. Dreyer requested that I give him a draft of what I transcribed. He usually changed words around and crossed out what he didn't want, and I then retyped the letter with no problem.

Mr. Byrnes, in the beginning of us working together, overwhelmed me. He chose to handwrite his letters. He had the worst handwriting I had ever seen. He did not want to use the Dictaphone. I had to decipher what he wrote, and it was trying. There were times that no matter how hard I tried, I couldn't read his handwriting. I then went to the office secretary and asked her to tell me what she thought the word was. Often, she was able to give me the word since she had worked for Mr. Byrnes in the past. When I finally typed the draft for Mr. Byrnes, I gave it to him for correction. As time went on, I became used to his difficult handwriting. I loved my job and felt supported by my bosses.

Mr. Dreyer once told me I reminded him of Mrs. Doolittle in my *Fair Lady.* I believe what he was saying was that he enjoyed my growth in my job as his secretary. I felt blessed that I worked for a boss who really cared and saw how much I gave my best to do a good job.

At home one day, Anne came home and announced she was moving out of our room. She had decided to go back to live with her father. She told me she was broke and needed to save money. I have to admit I felt sad. She was a great roommate. I could not have asked for a better friend. When she moved out, I struggled with the change in my environment. New girls moved next door, and they often stayed up close to one in the morning. I wasn't getting enough sleep. Then one day, I was assigned a new roommate. It turned out she was going to be with us for a short time. She was a law student studying for her bar exam.

Nancy was a warmhearted, friendly, and interesting woman. She studied all day while I was at work. When I returned home, she continued to study. One day, Nancy asked, "May I use your television when I am not studying?"

I said, "Yes."

What a big mistake not to clarify that I needed the television off at a certain time, since I had to get up early.

She started to watch television just around the time I had to go to sleep, but I was too embarrassed to let her know I couldn't sleep with the television on. My low self-esteem ran my life. Between the girls next store who stayed up late and my roommate watching my television all hours of the night, I finally couldn't take it anymore. I kept in touch with my sister Annie. I called her often. She was divorced from her alcoholic husband, and her son was one years old. I told her how unhappy I was living at Queen of Peace. She suggested I come live with her. I never expected Annie to invite me to live with her. I was filled with joy and I said yes.

Moving Once Again

Moving in with Annie was huge; it meant going back into Greenpoint, Brooklyn. I truly believed it was the right choice. It felt exciting to have the opportunity to bond with Annie again. Other than phone calls, I had not been around her that often. Usually, we saw each other during the holidays when we all gathered at my mother's apartment.

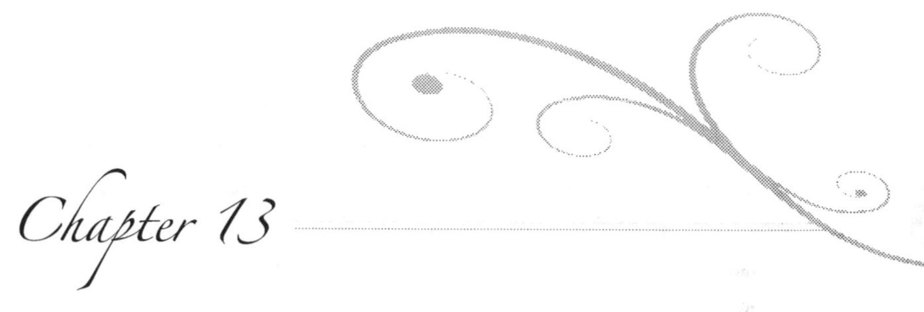

Chapter 13

I told Bobby I was leaving Queen of Peace. He agreed it would be a good idea for me to live with my sister Annie. He helped me move, and at that point, I was starting a whole new life living back in Greenpoint, Brooklyn.

I lived with Annie and her one-year-old son, Tommy. He was adorable, and I loved the opportunity to get to know him. We lived on Withers Street, Brooklyn, New York, for about one year. Annie was an angel. She had dinner ready for me every night when I got home from work. One day, I asked her if she would like me to give her some money for living with her, and she responded, "Ruthie, I don't need your money. I know you are saving for your future marriage to Bobby. Just keep saving."

I questioned her decision several times, but I wasn't going to force her to take my money. She was right. I was saving for our wedding day in the future.

Annie always was willing to give me the shirt off her back if I asked for it. Meanwhile, she was on welfare since she had a son and wasn't working. I helped out in other ways, and she appreciated having me live with her.

I loved seeing baby Tommy daily. He was adorable. I loved playing with him. He brought so much joy into my life.

After a year of living on Withers Street in such a peaceful, joyful environment, Annie informed me she was going to move upstairs from my mother's apartment. It was bittersweet news. I felt so content living on Withers Street, and we both enjoyed being together. Yet I felt it could be nice to reconnect with my mother and not live in the same apartment. I didn't know what it would be like to live upstairs from her. I agreed to help Annie pack on the weekend.

Before I knew it, I was living with Annie in another apartment building upstairs from my mother. The apartment had semiboxed rooms, and the place was bright and cheery. Annie's apartment was always immaculate. I had my own room. Annie and Tommy each had their own rooms. The kitchen was a big size and had good lighting with bright colors. Annie decorated the apartment attractively. She didn't like any extra things around the house. She hated clutter. She had beautiful taste.

I visited my mother frequently, and when she was in a good mood, I enjoyed it. She never hesitated to ask me to do errands for her. When I was able to, I did. Sometimes I was busy and couldn't accommodate her. But I never said no. If I wasn't available at the moment, I'd tell her I could help her out later. She had my older sister around, yet she always asked me to do things for her. If I put her off, she would express her unhappiness, and that always made me feel bad. Funny, I don't remember my mother going up to Annie's apartment. Annie and I always went downstairs to visit her.

A Scary Visit to My Father's Apartment

Once I had a horrible experience visiting my father. I never expected the visit to turn out the way it did. I walked into his neighbor's apartment, where we usually visited, since she had a living room and my father had one small room next door. I could smell liquor everywhere. He always wanted me to sit on his lap when I visited, but I never felt comfortable. Sometimes I did sit on his lap for a little while, just to show him I loved him and trusted him. But this time, I sat next to him. I didn't like the smell of liquor on his breath, and I didn't feel safe. At one point, he started singing a song that my uncle

Sydney used to sing to me. It goes like this: "I am going to sit right down and write myself a letter and make believe it came from you." I was surprised to hear him singing that particular song.

Out of the blue, my father looked at me and said, "Ruthie, you are not my daughter."

I stared at him in shock. I started to cry. I couldn't believe he would tell me that.

"Daddy, what do you mean?" I spoke.

He replied, "I am so sorry. I did not mean to say that to you. Please forgive me."

I left without saying goodbye. I was crushed.

When I got home, I told my sister Annie what Daddy had said. She was also shocked. We sat on the bed trying to figure out which one of us was not his daughter. I ran downstairs and told my mother what my father said and asked her if it was true.

She said, "I don't know, but I don't think so."

I thought, *What kind of answer is that?*

I went back upstairs.

While living with Annie, Bobby and I continued to date. Sometimes he picked me up from work if we had plans to go somewhere, especially on a Friday night. This particular week, when Bobby picked me up, we had an upset because I had hemmed my skirt, and he believed it was too short for work. I was so upset I asked him to let me out of the car, and I took the train home. My mother and sisters were going to visit my grandparents at Rocky Point, Long Island, and I decided to go with them. I loved visiting my grandmother. It brought joy to my heart.

When I got back home, I told Bobby I decided we needed space from each other. He asked me to forgive him, saying he was sorry he hurt me. Of course, I forgave him. I knew Bobby was sincere. I thought, *As soon as I learn how to communicate better, we will grow.* Bobby tried hard to show me how much he cared and that he was sorry he hurt me, and in my heart, I forgave him.

The one thing that bothered me most about our relationship was that I believed Bobby was more interested in sports and his friends than me. Sometimes it felt like he had little time for me. But I was in love with him. The truth is the lack of communication was our biggest problem. I lacked the ability to express myself in a positive way. I assumed we would grow together and learn to communicate as we became more mature.

The Big Question

One day, Bobby and I decided to go to the beach on Long Island to spend the day together. It was a beautiful, sunny day. I could hear the birds chirping, and the blue sky was breathtaking. I love being by the ocean. We enjoyed being close to each other. I felt happy and in love.

When we left the beach, we sat in the car, just talking and laughing. We were both hungry and decided to have some Cracker Jacks before we went to dinner. As Bobby took the prize out of the box, he handed it to me. He knew I always enjoyed the prize. I opened it and was stunned. I found a beautiful karat-and-a-quarter diamond ring. Bobby took my hand and said, "Ruthie, I love you and want to spend the rest of my life with you. Will you marry me?"

"Yes," I said. "I love you too."

We were both so young—I was just twenty. I decided that as we matured, we would grow together. I loved Bobby with all my heart. I was so excited to get home to tell my family.

My sister Annie was happy for me. She had such a big heart and was selfless with me. My mother and sister June were both happy. They all believed Bobby and I would get married one day, since, at that time, we had been together for four and a half years.

The Engagement Party

Both my sisters Annie and June worked in the Café 100 around the corner from our apartment. June's boyfriend owned the café. The family decided to hold our engagement party at the Café 100.

I appreciated how Bobby's mother and sisters came early to help decorate and make the place look beautiful.

Both families were present at our engagement party. It was a wonderful day. Everyone enjoyed themselves. I received many delightful gifts and appreciated all the love that was shared. Our families had a successful event for us. It meant a lot to us both.

Now that we were engaged, Bobby's parents allowed me to join them on weekends in the Hamptons. His father was a private chauffer, and during the summer, his boss wanted Bobby's father to be available at any time. Hence his family spent the summer in the Hamptons on Long Island, New York. Bobby's parents were always generous. I enjoyed the family atmosphere and loved being with his sisters and little brother.

And now Bobby and I were to start planning our wedding. It was an exciting time in our lives.

Chapter 14

Bobby and I decided to start searching for a venue for our reception. We looked at several places and chose Leonard's of Great Neck. It was a magnificent catering hall on Long Island, New York. It offered all we wanted to have at our wedding. On the outside, it had exquisitely landscaped gardens, with beautiful fountains. Inside was just as magnificent. It included breathtaking décor, with Bavarian-cut crystal chandeliers, hand-painted seventeenth-century-themed murals, and trumpet vine–covered trellises, blending elegant opulence with good taste. We went home and thought about it. We both agreed it was our favorite place. Now we knew we needed to pick a date in order to secure our space. We were told we needed to book it one year in advance.

Choosing Our Wedding Date

Bobby's parents didn't understand what the rush was for us to pick a date, but they were open to what we wanted. We decided we wanted our wedding date to be May 16, 1971. This date was available at the venue. We agreed to have our church wedding at St. Cecilia's Church. Since I was living back in the neighborhood, I again attended St. Cecilia's on Sunday. We had to secure our date at the church, and it was our next task. Thank God, May 16th, was available, and we booked it.

I asked Annie to be my maid of honor, and she agreed. I was elated.

It was to be a big wedding. All of Bobby's friends were in the bridal party. His sisters were my bridesmaids, along with my friend Sarah from New York, my cousin Carol, and my cousin Wendy. Bobby's little brother was the ring bearer. The bridal party was all set.

Finding Our First Apartment

Two months before our wedding day, we had found our first apartment at 1509 Greene Avenue, Brooklyn, New York. It was on the third floor in a family-owned building. The landlord was on the first floor, her daughter was on the second floor, and we were on the third floor. The building was kept clean and was well lit, and we loved the apartment. We had six rooms. We worked on it before our wedding day—painting, buying furniture and rugs for all the rooms except the kitchen. The kitchen was already beautiful with modern equipment. It had a self-cleaning oven, a garbage disposal, and a big, beautiful window.

We had six huge rooms. There were four railroad rooms. The kitchen was off to the left of the dining room. We also had a room off to the left of the master bedroom. It had its own outdoor entrance. Four rooms to fix up and furnish was more than enough, so we used this room for storage.

All the work in the apartment was done before we left for our honeymoon. When we returned, all we had to do was enjoy our apartment. It was beautifully decorated.

Our Decorated Apartment

When entering our apartment, we walked into the dining room. It was decorated all modern. Bobby decorated the dining room and living room, and I decorated the bedroom. He liked the modern look, and it was okay with me. We had deep purple rugs in both the dining room and living room. The walls had a molding design around each wall in the dining room, and we painted it purple and the background off-white. We had a white Formica table with chrome legs. The chairs were black leather swivel chairs with chrome legs. The hutch had glass shelves with chrome legs and a white Formica cabinet. It was beautifully modern. There were two windows in the dining room with long white curtains.

In the living room, we had two off-white love seats made of soft crushed velvet with chrome frames. The love seats were soft and lush. The end tables and the center table were made of glass and chrome.

The next two rooms were my design. One room was used as an exercise room. We had some wicker pieces in it. It extended into a big bedroom. The rugs were thick, plush burnt orange in both rooms, and the walls were white.

The bedroom set was my favorite. It was Italian wood with a very beautiful, simple design carved into it. It came with a magnificent men's wardrobe—a big Italian wood dresser with a magnificent mirror attached to it. We also had a king-sized bed, which I loved. We had two windows in the bedroom with long white curtains on both windows. The room was big, and there was a lot of space.

Our Wedding Day

One year after making the arrangements, on May 16, 1971, our wedding took place. It was the most exciting day of my life, next to my First Communion Day. I loved my white dress—it was perfect! It had Victorian sleeves and a beautiful Victorian collar with lace ribbons in several places on the dress. It had a beautiful trail. I felt like a princess.

My maid of honor, Annie, had a light green dress, and my bridesmaids had pale yellow dresses in a similar style to my dress, with Victorian sleeves and a Victorian collar. The men all looked handsome with their elegant tuxedos.

Mother, Father, and most of my family attended the wedding. Bobby's whole family also attended, and many friends. I pulled up outside the church in a black limousine. My father walked me down the aisle. I know he was proud of me and happy to share this day with me. I was so in love and thought how blessed I was to have this experience. When my father lifted my veil and kissed me, I turned to look at Bobby, and all I could see was the love in his eyes. My heart was full. The look he gave me is one I will never forget. The Mass was beautiful, and receiving holy Communion made the whole experience special.

Our reception was spectacular. Everyone had a great time. We took pictures with both families. Both my mother and father took pictures together. It was such a happy day to have everyone I loved present. We had a cocktail hour, and everyone talked about how delicious the food was both at the cocktail hour and the reception. The Venetian hour had every kind of liqueur you could think of to drink. The cakes, pies, and cookies were so delicious. The Venetian tray was filled with so many goodies I couldn't possibly remember them all.

Our Honeymoon

The next day, we flew to Acapulco, Mexico, to begin our honeymoon at the Las Brises resort. It was set on a hill overlooking Santa Lucia Bay. The view was unforgettable. The La Concha beach club was down the mountain. Dining at the club was magnificent. The food was great, and the atmosphere was fun and relaxing. There were many fun activities at the club, and we enjoyed some of them.

Our apartment was off the side of a mountain. It was big, beautiful, and nicely decorated. The view from the apartment was spectacular. The private pool was alongside it. We enjoyed eating and drinking by the pool. Each morning, fresh flowers were placed in our pool, and a continental breakfast was left at our door, consisting of fresh fruit with pastries and fresh bread and coffee. Part of the wedding package came with a pink and white jeep. We traveled in it to the beach club or to other restaurants, and it was so much fun. The honeymoon experience was magnificent, and I felt blessed the entire time just being with my husband.

But when we traveled into the poor area of town with our pink and white jeep, away from the resort, I felt heavyhearted to see how many children walked around with no shoes and lived in grass huts. The poverty was devastating. I cried. My heart went out to all those poor people we encountered.

After eight days, we left Mexico to return home to our new life together.

When we got back to our new apartment, all I could think was, *Wow, what a beautiful place.*

Chapter 15

Being married was all new to me. I had no idea how to be a wife. There is no instruction manual to use. I was twenty-one, and Bobby was twenty-two. I had not witnessed successfully married couples in the past.

I did love to cook, especially for my husband. I put a lot of love into it. I also enjoyed having dinner parties. We invited family as well as friends, and I often made my specialty of Italian dinners. Bobby's mom was a great cook, and I learned everything I knew from her.

Going to College for the First Time

I decided since Bobby was out a lot with his friends, I would do something for myself. I signed up to attend Baruch College part-time and was accepted. I had to make up a few courses that I hadn't taken in high school. I began taking algebra. I surprised myself and did well.

I took an excellent English course that made a difference in my life. The required reading was *Man's Search for Meaning* by Victor Frankl. What a profound book. I was required to write a paper on an experience that made a difference in my life. I wrote about my experience at Bankers Trust Company and how much I loved my job. I received an A as my grade. After the second semester, I dropped out of school. It was too much being married, working full-time, and going to school at night. Also, it was around this time that my father became ill, and I needed time to visit him in the hospital. I knew I would eventually go back when it was the right time.

When Bobby and I went on trips, we had a fabulous time. We took several trips to Las Vegas, Nevada, and always had a good time.

Once we went to the Playboy Club in New Jersey for an overnight stay, and I will never forget the magnificent décor of the restaurant. The restaurant was decorated with all mirrors, royal blue velvet and white. To top it off, the food was excellent. I had my favorite meal—lobster tails.

The next day, we played miniature golf and had lunch outside in a beautiful environment, then headed home.

Another experience I will never forget was seeing Elvis Presley in concert at Madison Square Garden in New York City. My neighbor and friend, who lived downstairs from us, had just broken up with her boyfriend. She asked me if I was interested in buying her tickets, and I told her I would ask Bobby and get back to her. I had heard of Elvis Presley, but that was it. I never listened to his music. Bobby jumped at the opportunity to attend the concert. My friend was a big fan of Elvis and was brokenhearted that she was going to miss the concert but was happy the tickets were not going to be wasted.

The concert was on June 10, 1972. Elvis came out in an amazing white outfit with sequins of many light colors. What an excellent entertainer! I was on the edge of my seat the entire concert. It was a packed crowd. All the women melted every time he sang. He was an amazing dancer. Every movement was sexy and mesmerizing. I believe this was one of his last performances at Madison Square Garden. What a gift our neighbor gave us. I fell in love with Elvis's music.

One day, I received a phone call from my father. He asked if he could come over to visit. By this time, I had completely forgiven him for the horrible comment he made when he was drunk several years earlier, and it had been an honor to have him walk me down the aisle on my wedding day.

Chapter 16

I felt excited that my father wanted to visit Bobby and me for a few hours. It was the first time he had come to our home. I was just beginning to become acquainted with him on a mature level. I thought he was intelligent, yet he never finished high school.

My father had lost his job in the past year. It was 1972, and he had worked for a bakery as a packer in Brooklyn, New York, for over twenty-five years. They went out of business, and my father never saw that coming. He was a proud man and independent as much as he could be. He was a union worker. The only kinds of jobs they gave him were jobs he could not do. The last job they gave him was working in a freezer. He couldn't handle it and had to quit.

While my father was visiting, he asked me if I could lend him some money. He said he had no money for food. I thought, *What a switch from all the years of me asking him for money.* His unemployment money ran out, and he was penniless. I gave my father some money. We spent a little more time together, we had lunch, and he left.

The Sad News

A few days later, I received a phone call from my father. He told me that he had noticed a lump on his neck and was concerned it might be something bad. I believe my father knew he was sick, but since he had no insurance, he did nothing about it. Once he saw the lump, he became frightened.

I called my sisters Annie and June and explained the situation with Daddy. I asked them if they would chip in for a doctor's visit. They both agreed. I made the appointment with my medical doctor and asked Bobby to drive us to the doctor's office. He agreed.

At the doctor's office, I noticed my father didn't look well. He had seemed tired the day he visited me, but I didn't think much of it.

The Doctor's visit

Dad went into see the doctor. The doctor took an ex-ray of Dad's lungs. When Dad came back into the waiting room, he said, "Ruthie, I am on a wagon train, and this is the last stop."

I said, "Daddy, don't say that."

When the doctor called me into the office, he gave me awful news. Dad had stage 4 lung cancer. It wasn't the type from smoking cigarettes. Hearing this news was shocking because as far back as I could remember, my father smoked unfiltered cigarettes.

The doctor told me I needed to get Dad into a hospital quickly and that he had only two months to live. The doctor said he would work on finding a bed at New York Infirmary.

Before we left the office, the doctor explained that my dad was put on a waiting list for New York Infirmary Hospital. The doctor requested that I take Dad to the welfare office and ask for a Medicaid card. I felt so sad and devastated that my father was going to die when I was just getting to know him.

I wish I had known that Dad was a veteran, but I had no idea. I could have brought him directly to the Veteran's Hospital. I told my father we needed to go to the Medicaid office to get insurance, and then I would take him home and wait for a bed at the New York Infirmary. When we arrived at the Medicaid office, there was a long line just to get into the office. Dad wasn't feeling well, but he was too proud to say anything. Eventually, he passed out. I became frightened for his life. One of the guards finally found Dad a seat, and I continued to wait in line. Finally, when a worker was ready to see me, I told her the whole story.

Dad was escorted to the desk. The worker asked for the information she needed and apologized for the long wait. I thanked her, and she gave me the card Dad needed.

Dad's Last Ride on the New York City Subway

I brought Dad down the subway, and we waited for the train, and I thought, *This is the last time Dad will be on the New York City Subway.* The sadness continued as a tear fell down my face. I could tell he was barely able to stand.

Finally, we arrived at Dad's apartment, where he lived with Elizabeth, an African American woman. She had been in my father's life for years, but it was only then that I realized they were living together. I was happy that Dad was not alone.

The next day, an ambulance picked up Dad. I met him at the hospital. So much pain built up deep inside of me knowing Dad had two months to live. I did my best to be upbeat, especially since I knew it broke his heart for me to see him this way.

In the beginning, I visited my father almost every day after work. As the days went on, I noticed he became skinnier and skinnier. Eventually, he was skin and bones. I had butterflies in my stomach each time I visited him. It hurt so much to see him this way. He couldn't hold down food, so he didn't eat much. In the beginning when I went to visit, he would be sitting in a chair, and I felt happy about that, but then he couldn't get out of bed. I always tried my best to keep a happy face.

Ruth Hostak

St. Rose's Free Home for Incurable Cancer

After six weeks at New York Infirmary, I was told there was nothing more they could do for Dad. They said they were finding him a home, where he would be taken care of until the end.

They found St. Rose's Free Home on the Lower East Side of Manhattan. Looking back now, I realize it was a hospice for the dying. But at the time, I had no idea.

My sister Annie and I went in the ambulance with Dad to the home. It was run by Catholic Dominican Sisters. Their ministry was to take care of the sick and dying. Knowing Dad was in this special place gave me some peace.

What made me especially mournful was that I was told I could only visit Dad twice a week. Sister explained that there was no way of telling how long he would live, and it wasn't healthy for me to visit him every day.

At this point, Dad was being fed through a bottle, and every time I saw him, it was sad, and I knew it broke his heart for me to see him that way.

The last time I saw my father alive was with members of my family. Uncle Hyme (my father's brother) was there with Aunt Jessie. Bobby picked up my mother and sisters Annie and June.

I was surprised my mother agreed to come to say goodbye, but pleased that she cared enough.

The day before my next visit, Dad went to his eternal rest. The grief went deep within my soul when I heard the news of Dad's passing the day before my visit.

We were able to get Schebelli and Sons funeral home to give Dad a proper burial, and I have no idea who paid for it. All I remember is that I invited Elizabeth to sit in the limousine with me and my sisters for the ride to the cemetery. I wanted her to have that honor. She deserved it, especially since she was Dad's good friend for years. Dad was buried at a veteran's cemetery on Long Island. He was fifty-eight years of age. It was too soon to say goodbye.

Chapter 17

Three years into our marriage, my cousin Tony told Bobby and me that he was moving from his apartment on Long Island into a house. He asked us if we were interested in renting his apartment. Bobby and I met with my cousin and his wife socially. Many times, we told them how much we loved their apartment. The only thing we did not like was that it was over a garage. But the place was huge and much more modern than our apartment in Brooklyn. The difference was that our apartment in Brooklyn had six rooms, and the bedroom was huge. In this modern apartment, the bedroom was small. Our king-sized bed and furniture just fit into it, with almost no space to spare.

In the living room was a built-in bar that lit up. The kitchen was big, with all modern appliances and nice-sized cabinets. The dining room was enormous, and our modern dining room set fit perfectly. The bathroom was an average size.

I loved the suburbs. It felt safe to me. I loved the beautiful homes and manicured lawns. We also enjoyed being close to Bobby's parents. My uncle Tony, aunt Jay, and grandmother Nellie all lived close to our new apartment.

Visiting My Grandmother

I liked the idea of living on Long Island and being close to Grandma Nellie. I loved visiting her. She was my mother's mother, and Uncle Tony was my mother's brother and my godfather. I loved both of them very much. Uncle Tony visited Grandma on a regular basis, so once in a while, I got to see both of them at the same time.

My grandfather had died five or so years earlier. Grandma lived in Rocky Point, Long Island, New York, all the way out on the North Shore. When my grandfather died, Uncle Tony moved Grandma closer to him. Visiting Grandma always brought back pleasant memories of visiting my grandparents when I was a child.

Grandma was a religious woman, and so was Uncle Tony. He picked her up weekly and took her to church on Sunday. Several times, I was able to join them.

Grandma's Miracle

St. Lucy was Grandma's favorite saint. As the years went on, Grandma lost her eyesight. It happened slowly, but eventually she couldn't see. She was told by her eye doctor that she was not a candidate for laser surgery. Her doctor believed she was too old for the operation. When I visited Grandma, she reminded me that she was praying to St. Lucy for her eyesight to return. Her doctor passed away, and Uncle Tony took her to a much younger doctor. He recommended laser surgery on both her eyes. The miracle is that Grandma was able to see again the last few years of her life. She believed it was a miracle, and she was grateful.

I visited Grandma as often as I could. I enjoyed spending time with her. I loved to pamper her. I sometimes polished her nails or fussed with her hair. She was often funny. She would say, "My home attendant took my favorite cup. I can't find it."

I said, "Grandma, why don't I look," and there it was, her cup in the closet.

When I told Grandma I found it, she said, "Oh she must have put it back." I would just laugh.

The day Grandma Nellie died at age eighty-three, I was sad. I loved her so much. I will never forget at the repass luncheon after the funeral, Aunt Jay gave me Grandma's wedding ring. Grandma had worn it for over sixty years. Even today, I wear her ring on my left finger, next to my own wedding ring. I think of her often and deeply appreciate her love for me.

My mother was grief-stricken when Grandma died. I stayed by her side. I tried to visit my mother more often during this time. Once, she opened up to me like never before. She told me that when she was younger, she had been raped. It must have been a painful time in her life. With Grandma passing away, it brought up many of her younger memories. This one was the only one she shared. I did not ask her for details because I knew it was difficult and painful for her. I tried to be there for Mother the best I knew how.

Bobby and I lived on Long Island for several years, and life was good. When we first moved to Long Island, it was the happiest time of our marriage.

Bobby and I talked about me quitting my job in Manhattan. I wanted to go to college full-time. My dream was to attend St. John's

University. Bobby said we could afford for me to quit my job, but we could not afford for me to go to St. John's University.

I worked at Bankers Trust Company for six years successfully, but commuting from Long Island wasn't easy. We both agreed it was time for me to do something else. I told my supervisor that I planned to go to college. It was hard to leave Bankers Trust Company. We were like family. They had a going-away party for me, and I felt special and loved.

I met my friend Paris at Bankers Trust Company. She and I continue to be friends today, fifty years later. She told me about a Christian awakening weekend where one strengthens their relationship with God. The awakening was held at St. Paul's Center in Greenpoint, Brooklyn. I was excited to participate in the weekend. I invited Bobby to join me, and he declined but was supportive of me attending. It was close to where my mother lived. This was exciting that I could stay with her at night and attend the event. I registered to do the weekend.

Around the same time, Bobby came home and showed me an article he found in a magazine. It was about EST—Erhard Seminars Training. The article talked about Dale Carnegie. Bobby had recently done the Dale Carnegie course for his business. He had started a men's shoe business and was open to becoming more motivated and successful. He asked, "Ruthie, would you be interested in attending one of the introductory sessions with me?"

I told him I would. I felt that whatever we could do to grow and expand our lives was a good thing. We both went to the guest event. We both loved the experience. We enjoyed everything that was shared with us. We both wanted to do the training. But the next weekend available was the same weekend of my Christian awakening, and enhancing my relationship with God seemed more important to me. We agreed that Bobby would do the EST weekend first, and then I would do the following course.

The Christian Awakening

While Bobby went to the first weekend of Erhard Seminar's Training, I attended the Christian awakening at St. Paul's Center. To my surprise, I knew the priest who led the weekend. Father Jim Tugwood was the young priest who served Mass ten years earlier when I attended daily Mass at St. Cecelia's Church. In my heart, I knew I was in the right place. Father Jim remembered me, and that felt good. He was always an inspiration. From the moment the weekend began, I had tears in my eyes. They were tears of sadness and joy. I again realized that Jesus loved me. I was his creation, and "God don't make junk."

The talks were meaningful. I appreciated how Father Jim spread out the talks so we had time for reflection.

As a Catholic, I was never encouraged to read the Bible. The only time I heard the Bible was at Mass. During this awakening weekend, we were encouraged to read the Bible, and I was given my very own. It was a modern version for young people—The Good News for Modern Man. This Bible was written so the average person could read it and understand it. This was a new experience for me, and I was excited about using it for prayer.

The weekend was a healing experience. I felt at peace and joyful when it was over. I loved sharing God with my mother, and she loved listening to me. She loved God, and when she felt good, she sometimes went to church.

One gift I always attributed to my mother was the gift of forgiveness. I shared that part of my weekend with her, and she enjoyed hearing about it. My mother was a forgiving person. If someone hurt her, she easily forgave them. I believe I learned that from her. It made it easier for me to forgive her for my poor upbringing.

Chapter 18

One of many gifts I attribute to Bobby is Erhard Seminars Training (EST). It transformed the quality of my life in every way. I did the two-weekend training after the Christian awakening. It was perfect. It was an opportunity to decide and get clarity on what I wanted to do with my life. Since I left my job at Bankers Trust Company, I now had a clean slate and the opportunity to choose what was next.

As the first weekend began, I had butterflies in my stomach, especially since I had no idea what to expect. Being in a completely new environment was a challenge. I enjoyed the dialogue with the trainer. I was at the edge of my seat listening to every word. The trainer began with the ground rules so that the weekend worked effectively. Many of the ground rules had to be repeated numerous times the first morning. I found it funny and laughed often at the way the trainer presented them.

One of the ground rules was to agree to go to the bathroom during assigned breaks only, unless one had a doctor's note that allowed them to go when they needed. I had to go to the restroom the first few minutes after the trainer went over that rule. He shared that going to the bathroom could be an escape when a participant did not want to deal with their feelings. It made sense to me. So, I had to sit in my seat and keep my mind off needing to go to the bathroom until the first break. The breaks were frequently given, so it wasn't too long before I ran to the restroom. Other ground rules were to be on time, check your watch or contraband at the door, raise your hand and wait to be called on before speaking, no side talking. Wear your name tag at all times in the room. There were other rules, but these were a few. We spent a lot of time the first morning going over the ground rules and people acknowledging that they had a watch they didn't turn in or had contraband in their purse. Eventually, it was time for a break, and the trainer said, "When we return from the break, we will start the training." If someone did not want to commit to the rules, they could leave the weekend and get their full refund back. When we returned from the break, no one had left the weekend, and the trainer announced, "Now we can begin the weekend." We were expected to keep our word.

During the weekend, I learned that the EST training was based on one's own experience. Also, if I allowed myself to experience my feelings, emotions, and anxieties, all the problems in my life would clear up in the process of life itself.

As Werner Erhard, the founder of Erhard Seminars Training (EST), reported, "The training was designed to transform the level at which one experienced life so that living becomes a process of expanding satisfaction." Werner always told us that the training was an individual experience, and as the weekend went on, I began to recognize that my experience of living was different from others'.

My Fear of People

The first morning, I saw clearly how afraid I was of most people. I also saw the value of putting myself in the training.

I realized how uncomfortable I was with myself and others. I was confronted with a low sense of self. I was a secretary among so many professionals. In the beginning, being with the other participants, I felt intimidated. But as the training continued, I met people who were authentic and real. I then felt empowered to be fully myself.

The EST training helped me be in touch with experiencing life on a whole new level. One of the gifts I received from the training was a more direct contact with my experience of the present moment.

As the weekend went on, I discovered that I could have anything I want in life if I am willing to believe I can have it and do what it takes to get it. I saw I had the opportunity to study, learn, and grow in every area of my life.

The Presence of God in My Life

During the training, I experienced how deeply the presence of God is a part of my life. I saw profoundly within my soul that I am blessed. This training had nothing to do with religion, but for me, personally, it did. I had just completed the Christian awakening, and that experience had touched the core of my being. I recognized the Holy Spirit dwells inside me, and I can call upon his help any time I choose.

Many of the exercises in the EST training were confronting but valuable. One exercise was a fear process, and what I realized during that process was how frightened I was when being with my father. I allowed myself to experience the fear, and it wasn't something I expected to experience.

I left drained.

Other exercises helped me begin to realize how much I lived in my head, in the past, instead of being in my experience of the present moment. Until the EST training, I lived my life being afraid of what other people thought of me. I had feelings of loss and regret that I didn't have normal parents. I felt embarrassed and ashamed of my past history and therefore had little freedom to express myself. This training was the start of me letting go and opening up. It was the beginning of a process of living my life freely and being my true self.

I also realized I had a choice to forgive my parents for their inability to raise me. I saw that it was the way it was supposed to be, and I could blame them or forgive them and move on. I chose to forgive them. I understood that there is more joy and freedom in forgiving.

The training was about turning one's life around. I was definitely open to that. After the weekend, one thing I knew for sure was that I was the cause of my life, and I had a say in how it evolved going forward.

Participating in Erhard Seminars Training, and many of the courses in the organization, has helped me transform the quality of my life in almost every area. The changes I was able to make seemed to persist and expand throughout my life, as you will read in the following chapters.

This experience was life altering. I was able to see my worth, and I came to realize that who I am makes a difference in the world.

My Mother and the EST Training

Bobby and I participated in several of the EST programs. Bobby became a guest seminar introduction leader. He had the qualities it took to be in front of a room and share the gifts of the training. As a guest seminar leader, it was requested that you enroll people into the training. We both thought it would be great to have our families do the training. So, we asked my mother, "Mommy, if we paid for the training, picked you up and drove you home, would you be willing to attend?" She agreed. I was shocked. I never thought she would be willing to do something so far out of her comfort zone. She completed the two weekends, and that also surprised me. I believe it changed her in specific ways. She seemed softer and lighter. At one point after the weekend, she shared with me (in one of the exercises) that she had the experience that she thought she never loved me. She told me, "I cried so much and couldn't stop. I am sorry I felt that way."

I believe the weekend brought my mother some peace. For a while, she seemed happier and more relaxed when I went to visit her.

Every once in a while, Bobby and I took Mother out to dinner, and she loved it. Sometimes Annie came along.

Bobby and I encouraged Annie to do the EST Training. We also agreed to pay for it. She said yes. I believe she was willing to give it a try since my mother completed it, and she saw how peaceful Mother seemed to be.

I volunteered to do security outside the room while Annie did the training. I thought knowing I was outside the room would give her more courage. At one point during the weekend, when I had security detail, Annie came walking out. She said, "I was asked to leave. I couldn't handle it anyway."

She left.

When she walked out the door, my heart began beating fast, and I started to cry. I knew it would help her in so many ways, but I had to accept it was Annie's choice. I continued to volunteer until the weekend was completed.

Around this time, Bobby and I decided to end our marriage. He had been a big part of my life since I was sixteen. We both cared about each other, but for reasons I would rather not share, it was time to move on. I appreciated the time we spent together and in time learned to accept the decision.

Paris, my good friend from Banker's Trust Company, was very supportive. She was there for me every step of the way. She introduced me to her boyfriend's best friend, and we hung out together. It didn't take away the pain of loss I constantly felt. But it helped not being alone all the time.

I decided to take driving lessons since I was now a single woman living on Long Island. As I completed my lessons, I took the road test and passed it on the first try. It was another miracle in my life.

Since I was separated from Bobby, I decided to participate as a volunteer around the EST programs. It was a great place for me to grow and discover who I was as a single woman. I found myself spending a lot of my free time in Manhattan participating at the EST center. It fulfilled me in so many ways. I discovered how much

I enjoyed contributing to others and making a difference. I met the most incredible people, who were kind and generous to me, and I wasn't alone.

Meeting Barbara

I was attending a weekly seminar called "What's So." Basically, we were looking at what it was that we said we wanted in our lives. While attending this seminar, I decided that one thing I really wanted was to move into Manhattan, so I could be closer to my job and my volunteer work.

The first day of the seminar, I met Barbara. Meeting her filled my heart with joy. Barbara was one of the girls I remembered from the orphanage. She was in my sister Annie's group. It was exciting to see her. We agreed to get together the next weekend.

Getting together with Barbara at her apartment was exciting. To my surprise, she also had another friend visiting. Debbie was also raised in the orphanage and a friend of my sister Annie's. I always liked Debbie. Both Barbara and Debbie looked great, and we had so much to share.

When I mentioned I wanted to move into Manhattan, Barbara suggested I come and stay with her for several months while I looked for an apartment. I felt so grateful that she would offer her home to me after not seeing me since we were children. I told her I would love to live with her. I slept on Barbara's couch. She was kind and generous.

My First Apartment as a Single Woman

Two months later, I found a great apartment on Thirty-Sixth Street and Third Avenue, New York City, for $210 a month. This was my first apartment. I loved my studio apartment. Describing the apartment brings back so many good memories and some sad. As I entered, a big closet was on my left. I then walked down a long hall, and a small bathroom was on my left, and the kitchen on the right. They were both quite small but perfect for me. The main room was large. I had a brown crushed velvet carpet installed. The one wall to the left of the entrance was all exposed brick with a brick fireplace, and it worked. Near the entrance of the hallway also to my left was a cute kitchen set with two chairs. To my right was a huge wardrobe with draws. The brown and beige pull-out couch was opposite the fireplace. The bed was comfortable. There were two windows the other side of the room with nice white curtains. A large wall unit that was used for my stereo and television was in between the windows. I enjoyed having my very own apartment.

I lived a few blocks from the EST office. I loved it because I enjoyed being in programs and volunteering my time. It was a healing place for me. I have always told people that the EST organization gave me my life. I met professional people I normally would not have met. In spite of the pain and loss I felt deep inside my core, I was beginning to enjoy my life again. I had to find a job now that I was settled in Manhattan.

Through my participation in EST programs, I began to develop a good sense of self, and I knew I would find the right job. I went to an employment agency, and I found a job at Wainwright Securities as a secretary to Mr. Schwartz, vice president, at 245 Park Avenue. It was walking distance from my apartment. I loved my job, and I enjoyed working for my boss.

I lived successfully in my new apartment for about one year, until two very painful events happened. I stayed overnight with my friend Paris in Queens, New York. When I returned home the next day, I found that my apartment had been burglarized. Thank God, I hadn't been home. My diamond engagement ring had been stolen, and a huge jar filled with quarters, dimes, and nickels had been taken. My camera, a new stereo system, my television, and all my jewelry had disappeared. I couldn't believe how violated I felt. I had to call the police and file a report.

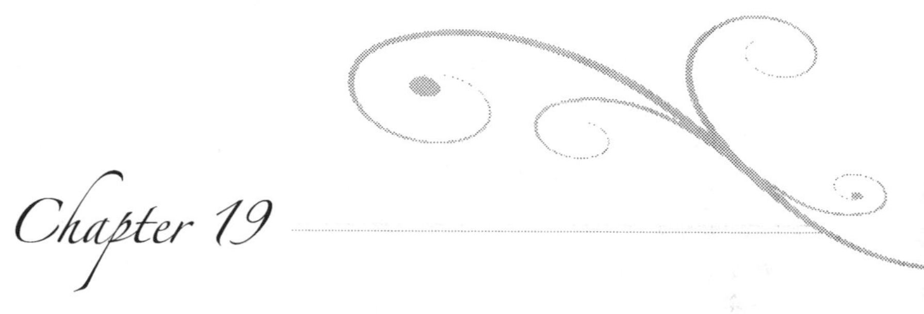

Chapter 19

The second painful event that took place around this time involved my sister Maryann.

One time, Bobby's mom and dad were participating in the EST training, and I had chosen to volunteer during their weekend. At this time, I still felt a deep connection to Bobby. He sometimes called me to see how I was doing. My sisters had been trying to call me. I didn't have a cell phone in 1976. They called Bobby to ask him if he could contact me. Oh, yes, we remained friends since we often saw each other at the EST center. And the truth is I never stopped loving him.

The News of My Sister Maryann's Death

Bobby came to tell me my sister Maryann died. I couldn't believe it. She took her life, along with a girlfriend at a motel in Queens, New York. My first reaction was disbelief. Then I broke down crying. I couldn't stop until I realized I had to get it together before I called my family.

Maryann was twenty-one. She often told me she wasn't going to live past twenty-one. I never thought she was serious or that she would take her own life.

Maryann had lost her father, Jimmy Babino, when she was ten years old. My mother worked full-time and didn't have much time for her. I wish I could have been there for her more. I believe she didn't feel wanted or accepted by many people.

Maryann's Short Time in a Group Home

Maryann once reached out to me for help. I brought her to a group home in Manhattan so that she could go back to school. She stayed several months, and I visited her often. I tried to be a good big sister, but I didn't understand her. My mother called her up and asked her to come back home, and she left the group home, even though she was doing well in school. I asked her why she chose to leave.

"I miss my family," she said. "I felt lonely at the group home."

Another time, Maryann asked me if she could live with me. I had the small studio apartment and didn't have room for her. I told her she could visit or stay over whenever she needed to, but the apartment wasn't big enough for her to live with me. For a long time, I felt so bad that I said no to her.

The Thanksgiving Tragedy

Thanksgiving was the day before this tragedy happened. Maryann called my mother's apartment to ask if she could come over for Thanksgiving, and she was told no. I just recently heard this story but am not willing to give details. But hearing it hurt me deeply. I cannot judge anyone because Maryann made her own choices, and she decided to take her life.

Even today, many years later, I still have the article from the *New York Post* written on November 30, 1976. It was heartbreaking to see a picture of my sister on page 3.

The Story of Rose

My sister was good friends with Rose, but at this time, Maryann was her maid. The article was mostly focused on Rose, who lived in Forest Hills, New York, and had men support her. For Maryann,

Rose's drug-filled world was glamorous. The paper reported that Maryann had been six weeks' pregnant when she died. Her boyfriend, Brian, wanted nothing to do with her when she told him about the pregnancy. I believe his response was part of the reason she took her life.

The article reported, "At twenty-one, Maryann died. Her partly decomposed body found clad in a brown jumpsuit, face-up on the double bed next to Rose. In a joint suicide note, Maryann said: 'I love you, Ma'."

Maryann confessed she was pregnant. She wanted her sister Connie to have her dog. She asked to be buried with her tarot cards in the coffin and her body dressed in white. The Queens medical examiner's office reported that the two women died Friday evening from an overdose of "potent barbiturates."

As soon as I heard the news, I went to Brooklyn to be with my mother and sisters. My mother was distraught, sitting at the kitchen table. My sisters Annie, June, and Connie were also present. We sat talking about how sad we were that none of us could reach Maryann and help her with her problems. We looked at pictures to pick some for the funeral. Maryann's body quickly decomposed, due to the fact that she wasn't used to taking so many drugs at one time, so the plan was to have a closed coffin.

Fulfilling my Sister Maryann's Dream

I decided to fulfill one of Maryann's dreams by giving her my beautiful white wedding dress. Because her body was so decomposed, they had to lay the dress on top of her. My desire to give Maryann her one wish, to be dressed in white, made it easy to give up my dress. Also, it was my way of beginning to let go of Bobby.

A few days after this experience, I wrote to Werner Erhard, the founder of EST. I shared that I was making a commitment to myself. I told him about Maryann's death and that it was a wake-up call for me. I told Werner that Maryann gave me life through her death. From that day on, I promised to work toward my dreams and to never give up on myself. I kept that promise.

Werner encouraged his participants to write to him. Since I did so much volunteer work, it was important for me to write. I loved it when he wrote back. December 10, 1976, Werner wrote, "Dear Ruthie: Thank you for letting me know about your sister and for your open sharing. I acknowledge you for being responsible about your experience and I am moved by your willingness to choose. You are great and I love you and support you totally in your experience. Love, Werner."

Werner was always inspirational. I loved it when I had the opportunity to be around him. Once at a workshop, Werner made a statement that transformed my life in so many ways. He said, "If you want to have a great life, serve one who serves." I remembered how much the Catholic Church did for me when I needed them the most, and I thought, *It is my opportunity to give back. I will wait for the right moment to serve.*

Chapter 20

I went to a holiday party in 1977 and met a friend who told me that he worked with street kids and runaways at Covenant House "Under 21," a crisis center in Times Square. It was run by a Franciscan priest named Father Bruce Ritter, who was the director of the program.

The center had just recently opened, and volunteers were needed. My friend's sharing inspired me. This was my opportunity to give back.

Becoming a Volunteer

Once I received the information about volunteering, I signed up for the training class and became a part-time volunteer twice a week on Tuesday night and Saturdays, for six months. It was a commitment that gratified me. I either did intakes or escorted a child home or to a hospital. I also helped with meals, cleanup, bedtime, or just listened to the youth who wanted to talk.

When my shift was over, not only did I feel grateful for the opportunity to serve, I also appreciated my own life more. My heart was full of gratitude. My own problems, or pain, seemed like nothing compared to the heartbreak of these young people.

Working in the kitchen, helping with lunch preparation and cleanup, was one of my favorite jobs. Doing service for these poor, abandoned children brought meaning to my life. It made me feel that I was making a difference.

At times, I invited several of the young people to help clean up the kitchen. They enjoyed helping. It allowed them to feel that they were important. Most of the young people were starving for acknowledgment. Whenever I had the opportunity to share something positive, I did just that.

The center stayed open twenty-four hours a day. When a young person entered, the first person they met was the on-call staff member. Each child who came through our door was welcomed, then given something to eat, and afterward, an intake interview was conducted. During an intake interview, we asked questions to help determine if the child was age appropriate for the program. It wasn't long before I could write progress notes and do assessments. A boy or girl under twenty-one could come into the center at any time of the day or night for help. They had access to food, shelter, a shower, clothing, and protection. The next day, a counselor would attempt to get enough information in order to help the youth or, though it was rare, even determine if there was a chance for him or her to go home again. Father Bruce once said, "A lot of these kids feel they have nothing to live for and wish they were dead."

The EST Holiday Project at Under 21

On Christmas Day of 1977, I brought a group of volunteers from the EST (Erhard Seminars Training) Holiday Project to the center. It was so much fun. I dressed like a clown, and we brought gifts for all the young people and provided entertainment. Marge Crawford, the volunteer coordinator for the center, shared with me that Father Bruce told her it was a wonderful Christmas Day. Without mentioning my name, Father Bruce wrote in the monthly newsletter that "there was a rather talented clown cavorting about the premises." It was just another opportunity for me to show these young people that they were important. I brought the EST Holiday Project to the center every Christmas until 1981.

The center was located on Eighth Avenue between Forty-Third and Forty-Fourth Streets—one of the worst and most depraved areas in New York City, definitely not a good place to live. At the time, it was estimated that the sex industry was doing at least a billion dollars a year in business within a several block radii of the Under 21 center. Pimps controlled thousands of girls, and it was believed to have the highest crime rate of any section of the city.

While volunteering, I became aware of the fact that there were thousands of homeless kids who were abused and/or abandoned. If not for Under 21, children as young as eight or nine years old were on the street with nowhere else to go. In order to survive, these young people chose to prostitute themselves. There were at least five thousand young people who came through the doors of Under 21 that year, many young people having been abused, beaten, and raped. A high number of these youth were from African American or Puerto Rican backgrounds and had no place to live. These young people were often thrown out of their homes or had to run away. Numerous white kids from other states thought they would find a good time in New York City, but when they arrived at the Port Authority, pimps wasted little time manipulating these young people into prostitution. Other predators singled them out, and they were robbed and left broke and stranded.

Covenant House Community

Covenant House is more than a shelter for children under twenty-one; it's a mission run by a group of Christians of all ages, living and praying together with a common purpose. These Christians were committed to spending a year of their lives serving the poor simply because they understood the need and wanted to help. They left their normal surroundings and dedicated their lives to God by doing this work with street kids who ended up in the challenging Times Square area.

I met several of these community members while being a part-time volunteer. At first, I thought being a community member would be perfect for someone just getting out of college but not for me. I was living in a great apartment on the East Side of Manhattan, working as a secretary for a vice president during the day, and attending Baruch College at night. These were definitely obstacles to consider.

One day, I received a call from a friend telling me to turn on the television. When I did, Father Bruce Ritter was speaking. He said, "If I as a priest don't help these kids, who will?"

His words touched me deeply, and before I knew it, I found myself seriously considering the possibility of joining the Covenant House community. I knew in my heart if I was being called by the Holy Spirit, I would find a way.

How Covenant House Got Started

When I heard Father Bruce share how Covenant House got started, I was deeply touched and inspired and knew I wanted to do more. His story immediately reminded me of the orphanage and the sisters who had taken such good care of me. Apparently, Father Bruce was living and teaching in a middle-class neighborhood just north of New York City when his students confronted and challenged him to practice what he preached with regard to caring for the poor. He accepted their challenge and got permission to relocate to a tenement building on the Lower East Side of Manhattan. One night, some kids found out he was a priest and asked him if it was possible to sleep on his floor. He agreed to let the kids stay and gave the boys food and blankets. The next morning, it was freezing cold and snowing outside. One kid left for just a few minutes and brought back four more kids, saying, "This is the rest of us." When Father Bruce asked where they had previously been staying, he learned the boys were occupying one of the abandoned buildings on the block, but it had been burned out the night before by junkies. Father Bruce thought he could solicit help for these kids but soon discovered, after contacting various childcare agencies, that no one wanted to help. The kids were either too old or not eligible for one reason or another.

While contemplating whether or not to live and work in the community, I was informed by my employer that Wainwright Securities had decided to close their doors. My boss asked me to stay on for a few more weeks, which allowed me the time to sublet my apartment and the freedom to enter the community.

Community living was definitely a new experience. I shared an apartment around the corner from the center on Forty-Fourth Street and Eighth Avenue with Celine, Kathy, and Nancy. My tiny room had a bed, chair, and a small dresser, making it necessary for me to bring only items that were absolutely essential for the year. The rest of my belongings were given away or put in storage. Eventually, the storage place closed, and my belongings were never returned.

After living in the community for one month, I was interviewed by Father Bruce. After completing my interview, the policy was to leave the community while a discernment process took place.

Entering the Covenant House Community

Two weeks later, I received the incredible news. March 1, 1978, became my official arrival date to enter the community. My emotions were running rampant, truly a double-edged sword of excitement and fear, but everyone's warm attitudes made me feel comfortable and welcomed. Also, having known several other community members while I volunteered part-time made the transition into community life a bit easier.

While I was preparing to enter the community, Father Bruce requested that I have a spiritual director, and, upon my request, Father Jim Tugwood from my Christian awakening weekend agreed to take on this role.

Some of the men and women who were full-time volunteers

living in the community were young college graduates handpicked by Father Bruce. It was different for me, a divorced woman and a high school graduate in my late twenties. Everyone was open and friendly. I found myself developing several long-term friendships with community members.

Deborah and I became close. She was in the community for the month during her discernment process, and during that time, we had many meaningful conversations. She met with Father Bruce at the end of the month, and they both agreed that it would be inappropriate for her to join the community.

I was surprised and disappointed. She was such a great person who was committed to serving the poor, and she proved it. She lived with an elderly lady who needed a companion, and she continued volunteering full-time in the center, cooking lunch and dinner. She worked hard and loved it. Whenever I had free time, I spent time with Deborah. Our friendship continued, and seven months later, I was the maid of honor at her wedding to Ed.

Deborah discussed with me what my plans were for living when I left the community, since I had given up my apartment. I told her my thoughts about living with my mother. She said, "Ruthie, if you ever need a place to live, you can always live with me and Ed. We would love to have you."

I also enjoyed getting to know Nancy and Tom. Nancy was a fun person whose enthusiasm I really appreciated. She was a blessing in my life because of her open and friendly nature, which allowed us to have a special closeness. Tom was a wonderful friend as well. We shared meaningful times together as we sat around in our living room while either Nancy or Tom played their guitar as we sang songs. I enjoyed those times and still treasure the memories. As their time in the community came to a close, they invited me to be in their wedding party. I am happy to say that we are still good friends today.

I bonded with Father George Aschenbrenner, SJ, who was another special person I met while he was visiting his seminarians at the Covenant House community during their internship process.

One day, Father George and I went for a walk, and I shared with him my experience at Covenant House. He told me he thought my desire to serve God was wonderful, and he reminded me how much God loves me for doing it. He gave me spiritual support, and his openness and willingness to share his deep love and commitment for God inspired me. He demonstrated the true essence of who Jesus Christ is in the world. Father George was a holy, humble, and compassionate man who lived by example through his work with other priests and seminarians. I have been writing to him for over thirty years, and he has always responded. His life has been a constant reminder of true Christian service, and it has taught me how to know God even more. I was reminded of God's love. It was an honor to be Father George's friend. I received spiritual nurturing from him.

I loved living in the community. We all had different schedules. Some of us worked during the day, and others worked in the evening or on the overnight shift. We usually worked four days a week in the center, and the fifth day we took turns making dinner. I loved making my favorite recipes. It was fun cooking for the other community members. There was always someone to help prepare the meal. We had a communal dining area and shared the living, sitting, and conference rooms.

At least once every other week, I visited my mother. Sometimes I had a friend from the community come with me. It was fun visiting her. She was always happy to see me. I tried to bring joy into her life whenever possible. One Christmas, I bought my sister Connie's daughter Francine, who was three years old, to our Christmas party with the community members. It was so much fun having her with us.

My Prayer Life

Having daily Mass, plus morning, evening, and night prayer, fulfilled me. I truly appreciated everyone's faithfulness to prayer. I loved the experience of praying as a community with the common purpose of helping the young people. I felt a source of strength and commitment I never knew before. Spiritually, I learned more than I ever dreamed possible. I loved reading the psalms and the office of readings from the Christian prayer book. Just knowing that most Christians were saying the same prayers around the world gave me a true sense of community.

Sharing God in prayer sustained my life in the community. I learned the importance of praying for others, especially the young people in the center. I experienced tremendous pain and tremendous joy and brought these feelings to prayer. I discovered a deep, intimate relationship with the person of Jesus through the scriptures and in the Eucharist. I loved to pray for family and friends and anyone else who asked for prayers. I felt prayer was another way to contribute to others.

When we were available and not working in the center, it was expected that we attend prayer and Mass. Our prayer times helped strengthen and prepare me for my shifts in the center. Community prayer life felt so right. It provided a comfort and sense of belonging similar to attending daily Mass as a teenager and the prayer life in the orphanage.

Father Bruce, as the director of the Covenant House community, often said Mass. He had great wisdom and concern for the poor, and I always enjoyed it when he was around. Community members took turns giving the homily, and I would usually feel anxious while preparing. I asked the Holy Spirit to lead the way, and then I felt the presence beyond a shadow of doubt as the Spirit guided me along.

Here's one homily in my journal that I shared with the community: "Remember how we were called to Covenant House to serve the poor? We started by seeing Christ in one another. We brought love with us to the center to serve the young people. Ask God to teach us a deeper appreciation of one another, and every time we think we are better than someone else, let us remember that without God we are small. Let us learn to be humble. God counted me worthy to join the Community and serve our youth and I appreciate it."

I was in the middle of taking two-night courses at Baruch College when I started my community life and was given permission to finish up the semester. It was almost impossible to study after a day in the center. I was tired, and my energy was drained. The semester ended in June, though it could not come fast enough, because it was difficult juggling both work and school. I made the decision to put college on hold again.

Working in the center, I experienced Christ dwelling among the kids. I responded with love and caring, with compassion and acceptance, and most of all forgiveness. At times, I was challenged beyond my limits to respond with open arms even when I was too tired, or not in the mood, or upset because a kid threw a piece of baloney in my face. Christ told us to turn the other cheek, and at times, I was called to do just that.

The work, by its very nature, was difficult and sometimes frightening. Yet it was rewarding because I knew I was making a difference. I loved the fact that the center was a true refuge for these broken young people. I was called to serve the poor and live in the community. It was this call that often sustained me. I had to be willing to be selfless, and in the process, I experienced what that truly meant.

The entire center facility was spotless and immaculate, and we did whatever was necessary to keep it that way. The kids were coming off the streets, and it seemed especially important for them to be in a comfortable environment. The young people deserved it. In the winter months, there were often so many kids in the center that some nights the youth had to sleep in the church. We gave out a mat and a blanket, and they found themselves a spot on the floor. These were always touching times for me, and I felt blessed to have this opportunity to serve.

Working in the center with troubled youth who felt unwanted sometimes brought up my own personal pain. It was a struggle being alone with my feelings; the tears came easily, especially during my private prayer time. I had uncertainty about my life, as I was dealing with the loss of my husband, Bobby, the pain of loneliness, and a fear of the unknown. I brought all these emotions to prayer. In my stillness during prayer, I realized how much I still loved Bobby, but I had to let go and accept that it was over between us. I always felt that he was more than a husband; he was family. We met as teenagers, married at twenty-one, separated at twenty-six, and divorced at twenty-eight. I received an official annulment decree from the church on October 10, 1978.

Whenever I was scheduled to work in the center, I prayed that the Lord would guide my day. It wasn't always easy to handle some of the males, but I gave my best. There were usually male staff members around, so I wasn't frightened. When I first began volunteering, I had no idea how painful some of my experiences would be and how often my heart would just break while listening to the life stories of young people staying with us.

I had been working in the center full-time for six months with no major upsets. One particular day, I had an experience with a young person, I will call Michael, that really challenged my commitment. I sometimes favored him by asking if he wanted to do cleanup, or I would invite him into the church during community Mass. I operated with the kids from a position of respect (i.e., I gave respect and expected it in return). I had a bad toothache and was feeling awful. I was sitting on a couch in the center working on a new intake. Michael was on the other couch, and he was coming on to a new female who had just finished her intake. I said, "Michael, be respectful and stop talking to the young lady like that." I told him several times to cool it, and then I realized he was more interested in coming on to her than listening to me. I finally had to get firm with him and tell him to go downstairs. When he refused, I said, "Michael, if you don't go downstairs immediately, I will have the supervisor send you out."

He wasn't expecting me to speak to him like that, and he jumped up and said, "If you tell the supervisor, I will get you for it."

I reported his behavior immediately, and the supervisor asked him to leave the center. Michael threatened me and later caused a huge commotion outside the center; the police were called, and he was suspended from the center for one month.

I wasn't feeling very well and was extremely disappointed that Michael responded the way he did. I ran up to the community in tears. The community members who were up there were supportive of my feelings and gave encouraging words that comforted me.

A Challenge to Keep My Word

This was a time of significant challenge for me. I knew my friend Nancy would soon complete her time in the community. Michael's behavior was frightening to me. He hung around outside the center and threatened me whenever I passed. Each time, I had butterflies in my stomach. It was a tremendous test. Yet it was important that I kept my word to commit a year of my life to serve the poor. I prayed about what to do, and eventually I learned to trust myself and surrender my fear.

Many years later, while working with mentally ill patients, I realized that Michael was not only homeless, he was also mentally ill. Eventually, he was admitted back into the center, and I forgave him.

During this same period, it was determined that there was a need for help in the office. Because of my secretarial skills, it was suggested that I work two days a week in the office and two days in the center. I agreed.

While working in the office, I had the opportunity to make follow-up calls. I checked two weeks after our youth were sent home from the center, to find out if they arrived and were adjusting. It was a sad assignment because all too often, they had not arrived, or it was not going well. Many of the same kids returned to the center over and over again.

I also had to contact volunteers when the center was short-staffed. It was a pleasure making those calls, especially when a volunteer was agreeable to lend a needed hand. I remember calling Dave, a Jesuit novice, to see if he could work the overnight shift. He was able to switch his schedule at the hospital so that he could make it. Seeing the commitment of these individuals to show up on a last-minute basis, even when it was inconvenient for them, made my job that much more meaningful.

I spent my overnights in the basement washing clothes, in the office doing paperwork, or preparing breakfast for the morning. But no matter how much I accomplished, it was never enough. There was so much more that needed to be done. Before long, it became clear to me that my prayers asking for God's help to heal these young people was, and still is, the most valuable gift I could ever offer.

When I least expected it, events associated with the center triggered painful memories and feelings of rejection and abandonment. Once, I attended the St. Patrick's Day parade with several fellow Community members. I was totally excited about going, but when we got there, I became aware of all the children who were having such a good time with their mothers and fathers. It brought to mind unpleasant thoughts of being cheated from having a normal childhood and turned such a happy occasion into something very sad. Inside I was crying.

I had been living in the community for almost a year, and it was an important time in my life to search deep within myself for the guidance to know where I was being called next. I knew I couldn't go backward because I had given up my apartment and lost my job. I needed God in my life more than ever.

I seriously considered going back to college full-time, but there were two major obstacles—where to live and how to support myself.

As the last few months of my year in the community were winding down, fear was ever present. Being in the community was a comfortable home for me, and many wonderful relationships had developed. The work I was doing mattered. I was connected to the daily prayer life, and it just felt right to be there. I had given more than I ever expected to give, and I had received so much more than I gave. I could no longer go back out into my life as a secretary. I was ready for so much more.

It was during a community weekend retreat at the Jesuit Center for Spiritual Growth in Wernersville, Pennsylvania, led by Father George Aschenbrenner, SJ, that I remembered I wanted to attend St. John's University. It had always been my dream, but for years I thought that if only I had different parents, I would have been able to attend. I discussed my desire to major in theology with Father George. I wanted to know what I could do with that degree and how I would best share my love for God with others. The first thing that caught my eye as I walked out of Father George's office was the St. John's catalog that was right there on the bookshelf. I showed it to Father George, and he suggested I take the catalog home, complete the application, and submit it, and I did just that.

I had been in and out of Baruch College in Manhattan several times throughout the years and had accumulated thirteen credits, but being a full-time college student was my heart's desire. This was my big opportunity, and my dream came true when I found out I had been accepted to St. John's University for the 1979 fall semester.

My original plan was to leave the community on March 1, 1979. After much thought, I decided to stay for another six months since I planned on starting school in September. It was recommended that I consult with some of the council members about remaining in the community, and my first meeting was with John Boyle. John was such an inspiration to me. Every word coming from his mouth was life giving. He was a living example of love and compassion for others. He brought his big heart into the center to serve the youth. John became a Catholic priest and went to El Salvador to serve the poorest of the poor. He was an extraordinary man, and I knew that whatever developed from our conversations was what

I needed to hear. He agreed that staying in the community was the right choice for me, and he fully supported my decision. I also consulted with Brother Tom Merrill; another community council member I held in high esteem. Our conversations had depth and always contributed to me. He also agreed that I made a difference, and it would be a blessing for me to stay. Not only did Father Bruce confirm that everyone was in agreement with my decision to remain in the community, he also acknowledged me for my work in the center and in the office. It was wonderful to hear and know that I was appreciated.

I went on retreat for a week, and when I returned to the community, I was refreshed and ready to serve six more months.

Many fun and unexpected events occurred while I was in the community. One night, I happened to be sitting next to Father Bruce while we were having dinner when a crew showed up from the television show *60 Minutes* to make a film about us and our lifestyle. *People* magazine also had Covenant House on the front cover. It was an opportunity for the public to find out about the importance of the work we were doing.

On July 23, 1979, I wrote in my journal, "There is a sadness within me. It goes deep. Lord, I know you are guiding me. You are a big part of my life. I realize that for me service to others was, and is, the only answer to true happiness."

Living in Times Square for a year and a half was a great experience. I believe I made a difference with young people. I felt sad that it was almost time to leave behind my community life, yet I was excited to start school. The impact of the whole experience was immeasurable.

While living in the community, I learned that God loves me under all circumstances and is present in my life. The single most important thing I received from my service to Covenant House was an even deeper faith and trust in God. This experience has been a constant source of miracles throughout my life.

While contemplating leaving the community, I had to decide

where I was going to live. I went to Brooklyn to visit my mother. I discussed the possibility of living with her while I attended college. She said, "Ruthie, I would love to have you come and live with me. It is a great idea."

I felt it would be an opportunity to make a difference in my mother's life by getting to know her as an adult. I felt I never gave her a chance to really get to know me. It would be a way of allowing her to contribute to me and me to give back to her. I felt excited yet concerned with how it would work out with my need to study.

Attending St. John's was a dream come true, yet I knew it would be a lot of work. I was beginning my first semester with four courses. I decided to leave it in the hands of the Holy Spirit.

Leaving the Covenant House Community

On September 7, 1979, I left the community a very different and transformed woman. My Covenant House journey turned out to be a profound blessing that altered and enhanced the quality of my life forever. I now had real clarity and felt passionate about starting school. I knew without question that I wanted to work with young people, and I was determined to do something that I believed would contribute to them and serve God.

Chapter 21

The day I left the community was bittersweet. I was excited to begin my new life with my mother, yet I felt comfortable living in the community with people of like minds. I was sad to say goodbye. Some I knew I would never see again, and others I knew I would be in touch with throughout my life.

Living with Mother One More Time

As I arrived at Mother's home on Jackson Street, Brooklyn, New York, I had butterflies in my stomach. My friends Robert and John from the community helped me with the few belongings I had accumulated while living at Covenant House for a year and a half. I appreciated their service in helping me. They borrowed the Covenant House van to bring me and my belongings home.

When I got to Mother's apartment, she gave me a big hug. I knew she was happy to see me, and I was happy to see her. Mother thanked my friends for driving me home. Robert and John didn't stay long since they had to get the van back to Manhattan. I walked them downstairs and said goodbye.

The first few months with Mother were wonderful. She tried very hard to please me. She cooked dinner, and I could tell how happy she was having me home.

Attending St. John's University

St. John's University was exciting. From the first day I walked through the gates of the campus, I remembered my dream and the miracle of being a student. For the entire four years, I remembered it was a dream come true. I will always be grateful for this opportunity. I began as a freshman at age twenty-nine. My first semester, I took four courses, which were required to be a full-time student. I had an English literature course, and it was difficult to understand. Mother enjoyed me reading out loud to her, and I appreciated her listening since it was the only way I could absorb the material. When she listened, I felt so much love for her, knowing how happy she was to have me home. The joy we shared went on for the whole first semester.

Another thing I loved doing with Mother was, on Saturday evening, we went to church for Sunday Mass with her favorite priest as the celebrant. After Mass, we went to bingo. It was so much fun. Sometimes Annie or June joined us at bingo.

My room at Mom's was in the back of the apartment. Mother gave me her room and moved into the middle room. I appreciated that. Actually, my bedroom set, from when I was first married, somehow ended up in Mother's apartment. I enjoyed sleeping on the large king-size bed. We had curtains that separated the rooms.

Life went along smoothly until the problems began in the building, and they only got worse. I wasn't sure how long I would be able to handle the noise. The lady who lived downstairs on the first floor yelled and screamed at her children all hours of the night. When I first moved in, it wasn't so bad, and I could tune it out, but it got worse.

My sister Connie lived on the second floor with her husband and four children. The children were adorable, and I loved being with them when I first came home from school or on the weekends. Connie had two girls and two boys. I became godmother to the oldest boy, Moses. It was great having the children close. But then

Connie decided to visit with Mother after all the children were asleep around 11:00 p.m. This was the time I needed to be in bed so I could be on time for school. I found myself becoming anxious and had a hard time sleeping until Connie finally went downstairs. Usually, it was after midnight, and I struggled to fall asleep. I mentioned to both Connie and Mother that I couldn't sleep with them socializing so late at night. They promised they would be quiet, but it never turned out that way.

A Tragedy at Home

One Saturday afternoon, as Mother left the apartment to go downstairs, I heard a loud noise in the hallway and went running to see what had happened. Mother had fallen down a flight of stairs. We had to call 911 to get her up. They took her to the hospital, and the sad news was she had broken her ankle. She was a mess.

It was the start of my second semester at St. John's, and I was taking five classes. Everything changed at home. Mother was totally unavailable to me, and she now needed all the attention. I tried hard to be there for her, but with my school load and much homework, I realized this was not the ideal place for me to be anymore.

I gave my best. I tried to be a good daughter. I did love Mother, but I also had to think of my life going forward. I needed to stay in school, and I didn't know what to do. Then one day I remembered my good friends Deborah and Ed, who made it clear that if I ever needed a place to stay, I always had a room in their apartment. Originally, when we had that conversation, I thanked them but never thought I would take them up on it.

I remained in touch with Deborah. We talked on the phone often. She was always interested in how I was doing in school. In her previous life, she was an educator. I had been telling her about the lady downstairs getting louder and louder at night and my sister Connie visiting Mother late at night. She just listened. I told her that since Mother fell and broke her ankle, I knew I couldn't stay with her anymore. It wasn't supporting my school life. When I told Deborah how upset I was, she reminded me that I always had a room in her apartment. I asked, "Deborah, do you really mean it? Could you ask Ed and let me know for sure?"

She said, "Definitely you can come. Just say the word, and Ed and I will come and bring you to our home."

The next thing to do was to talk to Mother. I didn't want her to think she failed me. It wasn't her fault that the building was too volatile for me to stay. Also, I knew she needed Connie more than ever, and I didn't want to make her feel bad that I couldn't sleep because of their visits. I explained to Mother that I had a lot of homework and needed more quiet time to study. I asked her if she would be upset if I moved out. I promised I would visit her and call her, which was something I did throughout her life. She was so wonderful about it. She told me she understood my need to move. At this point, Mother had a home attendant visiting a few hours a day who took care of her immediate needs.

Living with Deborah and Edward

I called Deborah that same day, and the next day Deborah and Ed picked me up and brought me to their apartment on Staten Island, New York. They were both great people, and I felt so safe living with them. When I wanted to give them money to contribute for food, they refused it. They told me I didn't cost them anything, and it was a privilege to have me around.

Deborah was a role model of selfless generosity. She was selfless in everything she did. It was peaceful living with Deborah and Ed. I loved the time I spent with them.

While living with Deborah and Ed, twice a week they brought sandwiches and fed the homeless on the Bowery of New York City.

Deborah and Ed enjoyed drinking beer; they actually met in a pub. They had a special place in their hearts for that population.

The only time they let me contribute money was on holidays. I contributed money toward the turkey sandwiches that Deborah and Ed gave to the homeless alcoholics.

As I said before, Deborah was an educator. Before she moved to New York, she taught at the University of Chicago and at St. John's in Annapolis, Maryland. She taught the classics in a tutorial program. She loved the classics and was a brilliant woman.

Deborah helped me with my grammar. She helped me with math and other subjects. She and I had the best conversations about religion and the lives of saints. She was from the old-school religion and had a deep faith in God. I loved her.

In order to get to school, I commuted two hours one way from Staten Island, New York. I took a bus to the boat, two trains, and a bus.

Emotionally, I had a difficult time. Everyone at school was ten years younger than me. I had to learn to accept it, and I did. I sought out counseling to deal with my feelings. I began to see Sister Maureen.

School was not easy. I first majored in health administration, but when I understood the job itself, it wasn't for me. I changed my major to theology. I actually wanted to study theology from the beginning, but a friend I highly admired and respected said it would be too hard. I felt called to it, so I decided to do it anyway.

I had to study a lot. I had a tutor for both Spanish and math. I did well with a tutor.

Volunteering with Campus Ministry

Participating in campus ministry brought me much joy. I felt connected with the other people who joined campus ministry. I took part in the World Hunger Walk on Good Friday. I did the walk every year. We collected donations from friends and family and walked ten miles. It was lots of fun. I believed I made a difference.

Volunteering with Bread for the World

In my sophomore year, I heard about an internship with Bread for the World, a hunger organization. For the summer between my sophomore and junior year, I applied and was accepted. For ten weeks, I lobbied in the Harrisburg/Hershey area of Pennsylvania. My job was to get people in the area to become more active with Bread for the World and, before I left the area, to create new leadership. The leader of the area was Tim. He wanted to step down from his position, and part of my job was to find him a replacement. He sponsored my ten weeks. I lived with his wonderful family.

While I worked with the members of Bread for the World, I met Paul. Paul and I became good friends. We shared our personal lives with each other. Paul often talked about his best friend, Paul Dermody. Several times, he said, "Paul Dermody thinks of himself as a loner, but all he really needs is a good woman."

I gave talks at the churches. Paul drove me to all my talks and meetings. I created a public speaking group among our membership. Since I never felt comfortable speaking in front of groups, this was an opportunity to grow, and I did. I often had meetings with the membership and encouraged them to bring new members in, and they did. The people involved with Bread for the World were committed to the cause. I appreciated Paul's help. I also created new leadership before I completed my job. I was successful with the internship and proud to receive an award for it. My commitment to the poor was featured in the neighborhood magazine and in the local newspaper. I learned much about Bread for the World and world hunger.

I lobbied in Washington, DC, at Shirley Chisholm's office to talk about homelessness. It was my first time in Washington, DC.

I received ten credits toward my junior year for the work I completed with Bread for the World. I was the only volunteer who received a stipend.

Paul wrote to me every once in a while, to let me know how he was doing in Harrisburg. He also let me know his intention to find a volunteer job teaching English as a second language to young people in New York City.

Once, while visiting Aunt Jessie and Uncle Hyme, I asked Aunt Jessie if I could stay with them once or twice a week to make it easier to get to school. Aunt Jessie said, "Yes, of course you can." It was just a thought. I wasn't sure if I would actually do it.

I mentioned it to Deborah, and she also thought it was a good idea. She let me know that she and Ed were thinking about moving to the Adirondack Mountains. Deborah thought it was time for a change, and I let them know I could find another place to live if they planned on moving. She informed me it wasn't anytime soon, so I didn't need to rush to look for a place.

One day shortly after my conversation with Deborah, I received a phone call from Aunt Jessie. She told me that Uncle Hyme was in the hospital. She said, "Ruthie, could you stay with me until Uncle Hyme gets home from the hospital? I have never spent nights alone and don't feel comfortable."

The Death of Uncle Hyme

I agreed to go stay with Aunt Jessie. The next day was Sunday. I went to Aunt Jessie's with clothes to stay for a week or so. I visited Uncle Hyme that same day. He had lung cancer, and his heart was failing. One week later, Uncle Hyme passed away in February 1981. When I heard the news, I wept. I loved Uncle Hyme. He was so special. It was a difficult time for all of us. He was such a kind, loving man with a big heart.

Living with Aunt Jessie Once Again

Aunt Jessie asked me to live with her, and I said yes. I went to Deborah and Ed's apartment and shared the news. They didn't mind at all since they were going to look at a house in the Adirondack Mountains. They were happy I would be living with Aunt Jessie. Deborah and Ed drove me into the city with all my belongings, and we agreed I would visit them during my school breaks.

The last time I lived with Aunt Jessie, I was eighteen. I never thought I would be moving back to the Lower East Side; much less be living in a housing project again. It turned out it wasn't so bad. Aunt Jessie was supportive of me, and we became close.

Deborah and Ed did move. During my vacation, I visited them. Deborah helped me correct the grammar in my term papers. It was always great to be with them.

While living at Aunt Jessie's, I decided to work part-time at Covenant House as a childcare worker. I worked when I could schedule to work. Usually, I worked a shift on the weekend, either Saturday or Sunday, and one or two evenings a week.

I believe that my life was led by the Holy Spirit, especially while living with Aunt Jessie. She made life easy. She did the cooking and cleaning. She never asked me for money. But whenever I got paid from my part-time job, I offered her what I could afford, and she accepted it with a grateful heart.

It was much easier visiting my mother while I lived with Aunt Jessie. Sometimes Aunt Jessie came along. She enjoyed going to Brooklyn with me to visit either my sister Annie or my mother.

Volunteering Once Again

As a junior, I continued to love school. I enjoyed being part of campus ministry. I joined the planning committee that year for the Hunger Walk. I participated in any opportunity I could to make a difference for others. During my junior year, I volunteered on Sunday morning for a complete semester teaching fourth-grade religion. The students were preparing for First Holy Communion. Father Michael picked me up at home and drove me home when class was over. It made this experience so much easier.

I also volunteered at the Blessed Trinity Church homeless shelter. I monitored clients and provided immediate service for overnight sleeping. For one year, I spent an overnight in the shelter once a month.

One of the events I am most proud of during my junior year was that I was awarded a certificate of achievement at the annual Dean's Convocation of St. John's College. I also received honorable mention for scholastic excellence in theology for my junior year.

At thirty-three, I entered my senior year. The first three years had been challenging, hard work, but also rewarding in so many ways. Now I was in my last year, ready to complete it all. My graduation from St. John's was one of the proudest days of my life. I had four sisters who never completed high school, and I was now ready to graduate college.

In my senior year, I had one horrific experience that frightened me to my core. Since I knew I would be taking Easter vacation and would not work the entire week, I took the late shift at Covenant House. I worked the four-to-eleven shift one night. While coming home that night at eleven thirty, I was followed out of the subway into my building and robbed. What a terrifying experience. It was a couple of days before Easter vacation, and I had a lot of books from the school library with me for my term papers. I have to thank God I wasn't hurt. The boy took my pocketbook and my book bag filled with books, stamps, writing paper, and more. I yelled, "Please don't hurt me. I just finished working at the Covenant House crisis center for youth just like you."

One of them said, "Just give us your bag, and I won't hurt you."

I felt terrified and gave over my pocketbook. I felt vulnerable and terrified all at the same time. Just like that, my pocketbook and my book bag were taken from me. I had so many personal things in both bags.

When Uncle Hyme was alive, he protected the building with the community center in the entrance, but at this time, it was closed. When I reached the apartment, I told Aunt Jessie what happened. She had to call an all-night locksmith to change the locks, since my keys were in my pocketbook. I reimbursed her, and I felt bad it happened. I had to cancel all my IDs. One of my checks were used, but I wasn't responsible for it.

When I returned to school the next day, I reported the loss to Father Freund, the chairman of the Theology Department. He gave notice to the library staff so I would not have to pay for the books. I deeply appreciated his kindness. Even though emotionally I was still shaken to the core from the night's experience, the next day, I attended the annual hunger walk. I then went on my way to visit Deborah and Ed for Easter vacation. Getting out of the city for a week was a true gift.

In 1992, I found out Deborah had lung cancer and did not want to see anyone. She died in 1993. Her death was a big loss in my life.

I was in therapy for the entire time I attended St. John's. It helped me with letting go of some hurtful feelings I held on to regarding the lack of a normal family life. Sister Maureen was excellent. I did meditations and exercises to forgive myself and others, especially my mother and father. I deeply appreciated having Sister Maureen as my counselor.

Because of my faith in God, I was able to forgive my both parents. I also understood that they both had rough lives. My father's parents died when he was nine years old, and he lived with his older sister. He had to quit school and go to work. My mother had her own struggles. Her father came from Italy and was extremely strict with her. He wasn't supportive or understanding, and it affected her behavior.

As I continued to see Sister Maureen, she invited me to join her prayer community. I thought it would be a great idea to be with other sisters. I wasn't sure what I wanted to do with my life and thought it would be helpful being around the sisters.

While going to the prayer group once a month, a conversation evolved. The conversation was about a layperson living with the sisters and how or if that would change the dynamic of the community. I was asked if I would be interested in living with them on Kessel Street in Forest Hills, Queens, New York. I agreed to talk it over with Aunt Jessie and let them know.

Aunt Jessie said, "Ruthie, I will be fine if you want to move in with the sisters. Why don't you give it a try and let me know how it works out?"

I thanked her.

Since the robbery, I never felt safe, especially at night in the neighborhood. Aunt Jessie knew that, and she said it would be good for me to move closer to school. Now, instead of taking two trains and a bus, I was able to take a bus to school. It was a great experience living with the sisters. If I stayed out overnight, which I sometimes did, they were fine with it. Once in a while, I visited my mother and went to church and bingo with her and spent the night.

During this time, I received a letter from Paul in Harrisburg, who informed me he was moving to New York City as a volunteer teaching English as a second language to poor Hispanic kids on the Lower East Side. He agreed to contact me when he arrived. It was exciting news. We were good friends.

When Paul arrived in New York, we got together for lunch. He invited me to a Halloween party on the weekend. He said, "I want to introduce you to my best friend, Paul Dermody. I believe you will like each other."

I agreed to go to the party. I let the sisters know my plans and said I would stay with Aunt Jessie overnight.

Moving Back with Aunt Jessie

After meeting Paul Dermody, his friend Paul was right. We both liked each other and began dating. I had thoughts of moving back with Aunt Jessie since I was now dating and didn't know how the sisters felt about it. I lived with them for six months. One day, Sister Maureen approached me. She said, "Ruthie, we enjoy having you with us, but if you plan on staying, we need to ask you to contribute financially to the household." I was surprised because money never came up before. I didn't have the money they wanted, and I thought it was a sign that I needed to move on. It was my last semester at St. John's, so I asked Aunt Jessie if I could move back with her, and she said yes.

As my senior year was coming to a close, I again received the certificate of achievement at the annual Dean's Convocation of the St. John's College. I also received honorable mention for scholastic excellence in theology for my senior year. This was another proud day.

As I said before, I will never forget how meaningful attending St. John's University was for me. My entire four years, almost every day as I walked through the gates onto the campus, I remembered how blessed I was to be attending. Also, I experienced such joy deep in my heart, realizing this opportunity was a miracle. I worked hard, and I loved the entire experience. It gave me so much faith in myself. I realized that I could do anything I set my mind and heart on doing.

We were coming close to graduation, and I never gave up. I did whatever it took to be successful, and my experience with Spanish is an example. I took Spanish I pass/fail, and I passed. Then there was the summer vacation, and I forgot most of what I learned in Spanish I. In Spanish II, I needed a tutor. The tutor moved me out of my fear, and I received a B. I took Spanish III pass/fail, and I passed. In Spanish IV, I received an A. I gave my best and never gave up. I had the belief that I could do it. But whenever doubt surfaced, I reminded myself that I am worth it, I deserve it, and I will do it.

My College Graduation

The big day arrived. I graduated from St. John's University in May 1983.

Aunt Jessie and Ruth—college graduation

During Mass before the graduation ceremony, I was invited to read the prayers of petition. I read in front of a packed auditorium. I had butterflies in my stomach. I asked the Holy Spirit to guide me, and I was successful. It was an honor.

I received a bachelor of arts in theology. In attendance were my sisters Annie and June and my nephew Tommy. Then there were Aunt Jessie, my best friend, Paris, and my friends Paul from Harrisburg and Paul Dermody. My family and friends were extremely proud of me. I felt so happy. This experience truly was a dream come true.

After graduation, we all went back to my sister June's apartment for a celebration. My mother was there with my aunt Jay and uncle Tony. The big surprise was that Uncle Tony brought my grandmother with him. It was such a special day. I loved having us all together celebrating my success.

Chapter 22

After graduation, I worked a summer job as a temporary secretary. While reflecting on what I wanted to do next with my career, I remembered I had been given an application to apply for a teaching job. In my senior year, there had been a presentation at school given by the archdiocese of New York about teaching, what it required, and how to apply. Applications were given out. I took one, never thinking I would apply. I had my heart set on being a youth minister. I interviewed a couple of times as a youth minister. The pay was so low I couldn't afford to live on the salary offered.

Since I knew I wanted to serve and work with young people, I decided to fill out the application and send it in. But I never thought I would get a response, never mind get an interview. I thought, *If I get a response, I will follow through, but I don't expect to get one.*

The facts are I had no teaching experience, other than being a student and my teaching fourth graders once a week for several months in preparation for First Holy Communion. I decided it would take a miracle for me to be chosen to teach. It was required to pick three locations to teach. I applied, stating that my only choice was Manhattan. Applying brought up the low self-esteem that sometimes reared its ugly head. A week later, I received a letter from the archdiocese with an appointment for an interview at Cathedral High School in New York City.

An Interview at Cathedral High School

Cathedral High School is the sister school for St. Patrick's Cathedral in New York City. In the history of Cathedral High School, the Sisters of Charity of New York were a big part of the school.

I was surprised that I was given an interview. I believe the fact that I volunteered at Covenant House added to their interest in me.

The day of the interview, I felt a cold sweat throughout my body. I prayed in the chapel and asked the Holy Spirit to lead me through the interview. Fr. Robertson, the principal, interviewed me and retired as principal shortly after he hired me. After many questions of why I wanted to teach, he asked me to send him a copy of my résumé, and he would be in touch. Here are a few sentences of the letter I sent Fr. Robertson on June 24, 1983: "My main reason for wanting to teach religion is because I know it would be satisfying and fulfilling. I realize that teaching religion is an academic endeavor and I think that an academic approach is best in the context of school. I also believe that the Holy Spirit speaks through all methods." I received a phone call the day after Father received my letter, and I was hired to teach ninth- and eleventh-grade religion. I was informed that I would be notified when to return to school for the teacher's conferences and for the start of the new school year. As I hung up the telephone, I began thinking of how this job was another opportunity to give back to the Catholic Church.

My Career as Teacher

I had to be at school by 7:30 a.m. Being at a job this early was a challenge. I tended to be a night person. But I did whatever it took to get the job done. I was committed to making it work, and I did.

As I began my teaching career, I held my job as an honor and a privilege. I loved working with the staff. Everyone was supportive and caring. We worked together as a team. If one teacher was absent, we took turns covering one of her classes. I tried hard to not miss a day, knowing other teachers would have to cover my classes.

The first year of teaching was difficult, getting adjusted to the format of teaching and doing lesson plans. I had to learn how to discipline the students and at the same time gain their respect.

In my four freshman courses, we started the semester by discussing the importance of getting to know oneself. We also discussed male and female anatomy, sex education, the meaning of unconditional love. The students learned how to put love into action even when it was not popular or comfortable. We explored and discussed the changes that take place in the life of a freshman high school student living as a teenager in New York City. Some topics were peer pressure, the media and how it affects our choices, and self-acceptance. I continued to volunteer and take seminars at EST (Erhard Seminar's Training), and I learned a lot of communication skills that I shared with the students.

The second half of the semester, we discussed the life of Jesus—the man who lived the example of unconditional love and acceptance.

For the junior class, the topic was social justice. I loved having the students learn about the causes of homelessness, the handicapped, world poverty, the environment, and the causes of violence. The term paper was such a great opportunity for the students to pick a topic of their choice, research it, and write about it. I enjoyed reading their reports.

My Job as Ministry

I loved my job. It was more than a job; it was my ministry.

One year, I had the opportunity to lead a Confirmation class in my free time. There were twenty-five students who received their Confirmation and two who were baptized. I was a sponsor for two students receiving Confirmation and a godmother for one of the baptized students. What an honor it was to have this special opportunity.

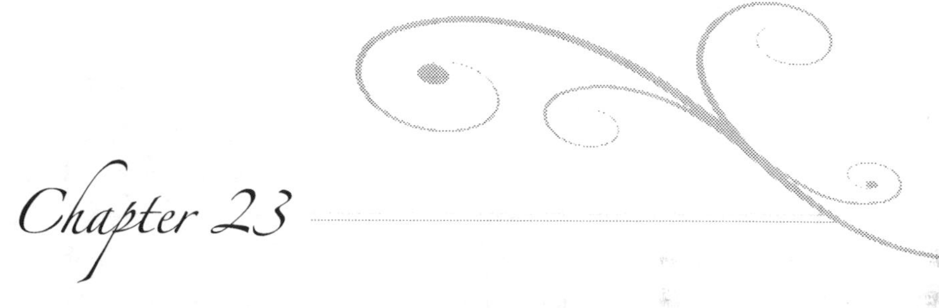

Chapter 23

Other Workshops That Helped to Transform My Life

Ministry Workshop

While teaching at Cathedral High School, one such program I participated in was a ministry workshop led by Werner Erhard, the founder of Erhard Seminar's Training (EST). It was an amazing weekend. I learned so much about unity and togetherness. Father Basil Pennington, OCSO, a Roman Catholic Trappist monk and priest, led the weekend with Werner. What a great experience of love and commitment. We had a rabbi and a priest serving the liturgy at the same time. It was a celebration of unity. My heart was full of love. I felt honored to be a part of this experience. I tended to put myself into environments that I knew would nurture me. This experience gave me a sense of pride knowing that I am an open person. Being in the presence of people who felt the same way made all the difference.

Many of the courses I participated and volunteered in over the years gave me the motivation to continue to dream big. And I do.

The Sterling Institute of Relationships

It was 1985, my second-year teaching at Cathedral High School. My good friend Paris wanted to share her experiences with a course she had recently completed called "Women, Sex, and Power." This course was given through the Sterling Institute of Relationships.

I had no interest in taking another course, but Paris continued to pursue me. Eventually, I agreed to join her and attend the guest event. As I walked in, I felt the excitement. Then came Justin Sterling. He was a stocky man with a big stomach and a powerful voice. When he spoke, he was given undivided attention from everyone in the room. He then gave us the purpose of the weekend. "The purpose is to engage in the process of locating the source of your power and discovering and dissolving the barriers between you and manifesting that power in your relationships and in the world."

He made some excellent points and gave excellent examples.

I was intrigued.

As the evening progressed, I thought about what I would receive from the course. During the break, I decided the experience would be worth the money.

As the weekend approached, thoughts of how much I had on my plate, if I really needed another course, fluttered in my mind. But I enjoyed my interactions with Paris, who supported me with my goals. I actually had to fill out my goals after I registered for the weekend. I had several weeks to work on them. When I looked deep inside myself, I realized I had been working on these goals for years but knew that it was worth going deeper.

My goals for this weekend were as follows:

First, to trust myself as the women I am, no doubts, no thinking my best is not good enough, and to bring myself consistently and fully to my friends, family, and my relationships.

Second, I will discover how to take risks and communicate better with men I find attractive.

Third, to value my women friends and bring more intimacy to my relationships by reaching out.

Fourth, to be in touch with my power and strength, to better enable myself to balance all my commitments successfully so that I stay focused on my career goals.

Fifth, to feel strong, centered, and at peace with myself and accept that I am good enough so that I stop settling for emotionally unavailable men.

Two weeks later, I received a letter with the dates of the weekend, March 8 and 9, 1985. The letter let me know the requirements for the weekend, what to bring, and how to be comfortable and get the most out of the weekend.

One of the requirements was to cook and bring a dish to serve eight to ten people. It had to be a representation of myself. At the time, I was living with Aunt Jessie. I decided to make my favorite side dish of stuffed mushrooms.

The Big Day Arrived

The big day arrived. I left my apartment with dish in hand, took the subway to the Upper West Side, and arrived on time. As I entered the auditorium, there were volunteers with colored name tags directing us. One took my dish and told me to get in line. I checked in and received my name tag.

When it was time for the weekend to begin, the doors to a huge room were opened on both sides as the women filed into the room, which consisted of a platform stage. A volunteer stood up at the podium with a microphone in hand, waiting for us to settle down. There were two sections of chairs with a middle aisle. In the back of the room were long tables with volunteers sitting at them. As women entered with enthusiasm and excitement, it took courage for me to walk into a room of unknown women. I felt butterflies in my stomach for the first half of the morning.

As the morning went on, I sat completely alert and at the edge of my chair. I did write a letter to my mother and father. I would like to share both with you.

Dear Mommy,

I love you for no reason other than that you are my mother. Even though I do not like many of the things you do. By your own examples of forgiveness, you taught me to forgive, and for that I am grateful. What I realize is that I have not learned yet how to reach out to others. I apologize for blaming you. My story is "my mother rarely reached out to me." I am willing to see growth in this area. I love you. Ruthie.

Dear Daddy,

I don't know if I am complete with you. I say I am, but I am not sure. You were an alcoholic. I never trusted you and was often afraid of you. But you gave me candy, bought me new dresses, and visited me in the orphanage. Because of this, I felt loved and had a sense of belonging. I struggle to belong now, to fit in, to trust. I want that. I know you always knew how much I loved you, especially in the end when I took care of you as you were dying of cancer. I know that you knew I loved you, and, Dad, what I want you to know is that I know you loved me, and I forgive you for the past. Love, Ruthie

During the lunch break, familiar insecurities reared their ugly heads. It seemed like everyone was together in groups with people they knew. Since I didn't know anyone, I felt like an outsider. It was uncomfortable, and I didn't like feeling alone. Both "I am not good enough" and "I am not important" surfaced. I was relieved when the break was over and I got to go back to my seat.

The weekend experience was profound in that I was confronted with my fear. I was also confronted with my lack of trust. I realized that in my personal life, I had difficulty letting love in. I had several good friends and family members who cared. Intellectually, I knew they loved me, but when I was alone with myself, I was not able to experience that love.

When Justin spoke, I sat at the edge of my seat, listening to him be confrontational, compassionate, and straightforward with women. I learned tips on how to be successful with men. One that spoke to me was in order to be in a successful relationship with a man, I first must love myself and feel good about myself. I saw a lot of growth in loving myself, but "I am not good enough" surfaced when I least expected to feel that way.

As the weekend went on, I remembered that I mattered, and who I am makes a difference. I also realized that failure from the past is not going to be any part of my present or future. I am a powerful, loving woman and have a lot to contribute to others, and I do.

Day two was just as powerful as day one. All during the weekend, Justin gave us tips for having successful relationships. The ones that touched my heart, I remembered.

The most powerful exercise in the weekend resulted in a huge breakthrough in my relationship with my mother. After the exercise, I realized my mother was never going to change her personality or way of being. She was not aware or capable. She did not know how to reach out. If I wanted a relationship with her, or to experience her love, I had to change. I had to stop expecting her to be different. Instead of feeling rejected and sad that she didn't call me, I decided to reach out and love her unconditionally without expectations. I loved her and wanted her to know it.

For years, on my birthday, there was sadness when my mother did not call. I felt hurt and unloved. After the weekend, when it was my birthday, instead of setting myself up for disappointment, I called Mother. I informed her it was my birthday. She was happy to hear from me, and we both sang "Happy Birthday." It became a joyful experience. I continued this every year. I realized if I wanted a successful relationship with Mother, I had to create it. I shifted my point of view and attitude. It was an opportunity to make a difference in her life, and I did.

Chapter 24

The Six-Day Course

I first volunteered in the six-day course, then participated in the course. I then volunteered two more times at Mountain Lake Manor, Kingston, New York. The six-day course was part of EST. Being a volunteer for this course was a course in itself. It was one of the greatest experiences of my life. I learned to let go of my fear and give myself fully. I learned to trust others completely. The most challenging experience and most rewarding was the ropes course. I jumped off a zip line. I did the Tyrolean traverse, and it was the scariest. I had to get myself across a pulley hand over hand. In the middle, it took every bit of strength I had to get to the other side. I also climbed down the side of a cliff. My first time doing this ropes course was as a volunteer. I was given the honor to lead a group of participants around the ropes course. After each course, we stopped and reflected on the experience. I enjoyed leading these exercises. It was challenging, but the support was amazing. I was willing to be in the present moment, let my fear be there, and continue to move forward.

For the ropes course exercises, all the participants went first. When it was my time to do the exercises, I let go of holding it all together and expressed my fear. The support I received I will never forget. The participants were at the other end of each ropes course, cheering, "Come on, Ruthie! You can do it!" I heard them, gave my best, and succeeded. This was one part of a week of exercises that helped me trust myself and let go of fear. When I returned from the mountain, I brought with me an unforgettable experience of my own magnificence and of the magnificence of others. I was also in touch with a profound love for people and my ability to be the master of my own life.

The six-day course added to my success in life. The organization retired the course when the EST training was retired. In its place, the Landmark Forum and the Advanced Course were born.

Being on the Six-Day Staff Part-Time

I had the privilege to be on the six-day staff for the last few courses that they planned to hold before the end of the six-day Advanced Course. I supported the participants to get to the course. It was such an honor and a dream come true since I always wanted to be on staff.

Another Opportunity to be on the EST Staff

One other time, I was hired during the summer to help out in the Graduate Seminar Department at the Landmark Education office. I helped participants enroll into our graduate seminars. Again, it was a privilege to be a part of such a great group of people. During this time, my mother was in the hospital again, and I was able to leave the office whenever I needed to visit with her. I appreciated the love and support of the staff. Mom was alone, and I knew if I didn't visit her, no one else would.

The Landmark Forum

The Forum was another positive transformational experience. As EST retired its training and the six-day course, the organization's name changed to Landmark Education and created the Landmark Forum in the1980s. I knew if it was anything like the EST training, I wanted to experience it. With the Landmark Forum came the Curriculum for Living and programs designed to bring about positive and permanent shifts in the quality of people's lives. I did the Landmark Forum several times throughout the years. I developed more confidence in myself. My level of personal productivity increased in my work life. I also became aware of the difference I make in the world. I realized that nothing from the past is worth fixing. To be in the presence of what is and choose it is a true gift.

The Landmark Forum was a dialogue, and it helped one to develop a natural ability to produce results and acquire skills. The Forum gave me a chance to experience my inner hopes and dreams. This process began when I participated in the EST training.

The Forum helped me to be more effective in dealing with my commitments. I am my word, and what makes that so is because I say so. My experience and practices of my faith deepened. It made a difference in my ability to relate to my family and friends. During this time, we were encouraged to write to a family member, and several of the times I participated in the Landmark Forum, I chose to write to my father. I want to share several of my letters.

Letter #1

Dear Daddy, I am honored to be writing to you. I am in the Forum, and I want to share the results I am producing. I came to the Forum to accomplish a breakthrough and a clearing for men to show up and date me. Actually, when I registered for the Forum, I did not admit my desire is to be in a committed relationship. I also came to the Forum to have a breakthrough in my ability to communicate my feelings and to ask for what I need or want. What I am actually accomplishing is a real sense of freedom in recognizing my life is perfect exactly the way it is. Daddy, the Forum leader said something important today, and it helped me to recognize this freedom. He said, "A year ago, you created the future that you are living into today."

I realize one of the biggest things I created is my teaching job. Also, being around Landmark volunteers and learning so much about accepting myself for who I am.

I realized that I have a say about who I am and who I will be, as the author of my life, in any and all situations. Daddy, I know how much you want me to be happy, and I know only I can generate happiness in my life, that happiness comes from within me.

I have always been afraid of you. I never understood why. When you wanted to hold me or when I sat on your lap, it was something I wanted with all my heart, but often I felt uncomfortable and uptight. I was actually afraid of the closeness. I am seeing that me being afraid of closeness is not limited to you, Daddy. I have been afraid of closeness with everyone in my life. I want it so bad, but when I have the closeness, I am afraid of it. When it comes time to expressing myself, I can better handle letter writing instead of actual contact. Dad, I have not until today realized that I might have been the cause of my failed marriage.

In the Forum, I realized that one of my rackets is loss, and the payoff is I make you wrong for dying on me before I got to really develop a friendship with you. I make Mommy wrong for leaving me. I avoid the domination of men. I get to be right that I am not gotten and men leave me. The cost is sadness and loneliness, lack of full-self-expression, and a lack of peace and centeredness.

Daddy, I forgive you for all the times you drank and I was afraid of you. I forgive you for dying. Thank you for always being concerned for me when you could be. I appreciate you giving Mommy money to feed me. I also appreciate you paying Aunt Jessie money when I lived with her and went to high school. I know, given your baggage and set of circumstances, you tried your best, and I absolutely love you for it. I love you. Ruthie

Letter #2

Dear Daddy, I am so excited I am writing to you again. It has been almost two years since I wrote. I love you deeply, and I want you to know. I wish you were here. I realize now that part of my fear of you being close to me was that it was unfamiliar; therefore, I had nothing to compare it to. I have always longed for a father, especially since you died. But, Dad, I finally realized I have a father, and I know you love me and want the best for me.

Daddy, nothing changed in my coming any closer to meeting a man to share my life with. I think my fear of closeness to you is directly related to a lack of emotional closeness to the men I date.

What I realized today as I sat in the Forum is that I have to be willing for nothing to change and embrace my life exactly the way it is. Dad, I forgive you for not being physically around most of my life. I also forgive you for not having an ability to listen. I forgive you the day I was sharing my feelings, and in the middle of the sentence, you told me to be quiet.

> I want so much to have good communication and full self-expression. I am intending to have a breakthrough in my ability to share with others and listen to others so that it further empowers my intentions. I am in the Forum, intending for a breakthrough and an opening for the right man to show up in my life. Daddy, I am choosing to be satisfied with my life exactly the way it is, with no alterations, and that is my gift to you. I love you.
> Your little girl, Ruthie

My Participation in Various Seminars

After the Forum, I participated in several of the programs. The Forum in Action seminar series was ten sessions, and it helped me to expand on what I received or learned in the Forum.

I also participated in the four-day Advanced Course. The one thing I remember from that course was I stood up on the stage and declared that "Who I am is unconditional love and acceptance toward all people." I have been living into this context ever since. I am not perfect, but I do my best.

I participated in many other seminars over the years. I appreciated being with the people in the seminars and the support I received. I held attending seminars as my entertainment.

My work with Landmark Education has provided much growth and lasting results that have expanded and unfolded over time.

While teaching at Cathedral High School, I continued to date Paul Dermody. We often visited my mother. Once on her birthday, we picked her up to take her to dinner. First, we stopped at Paul's house. We had this big sign in front of his house saying, "Happy Birthday, Mom." She loved it.

We had several opportunities to bring joy to Mother's life. She liked Paul.

Another time, Paul and I picked up Mom on her birthday. We were taking her out to dinner. I gave her a birthday card. She opened it and was surprised to see one hundred dollars. She looked at me and said, "Ruthie, why are you so kind to me? I never did anything for you."

I said, "Mom, I love you."

One day, I mentioned that I would love to do Christian service with Paul, and he agreed. I was excited to share that part of me with him. We began working at St. Augustine's soup kitchen run by the Missionaries of Charity in Newark, New Jersey. We helped with the lunch every Sunday for almost the entire time we were dating and while we were married. It was something special we did together.

Paul and I were married in 1986. Our wedding day went exactly as we wanted it to go. We planned the service together. We picked out the readings and the songs. I was the Eucharistic minister. It was such a special Mass. We had our reception at the Spanish Manor in our neighborhood, and all of our family and friends who could make it were there. Several of the teachers from Cathedral High School celebrated with us. We had a wonderful time eating, drinking, and dancing. The Spanish food was so delicious; everyone enjoyed it. The leftover food was brought to a soup kitchen. The next day, we left for our honeymoon.

When we began our marriage, I commuted from New Jersey to Manhattan daily to my job at Cathedral High School. The commute was a lot, but at the beginning, it was worth it. I found an express bus that took me directly into Manhattan.

Paul and I were divorced three years later in 1989. He is a good man but not the right man for me. I am sorry things didn't work out. When I take responsibility for the divorce, I realize that at the time, I still did not know how to have a successful marriage. It took a lot of future self-help courses to discover where I was the cause in the matter of our failed marriage. I know it takes two for a successful marriage, but I can only share my part.

Attending Graduate School at St. John's University

While attending graduate school at St. John's University in 1986, I was approved to do an independent study abroad in Israel. My assignment was to discover if the presence of Jesus was alive in the Holy Land, or was it mostly commercialism or secular tourism? I found the whole experience life giving. I took lots of slides of the holy places as part of my study. I used the slides often in my classes to share them with the students.

I worked successfully at Cathedral High School for nine years. I loved my job, and every evaluation I received was good to very good.

It was always inspiring when, every year at graduation time, I had the opportunity to wear my cap and gown from St. John's University. The teachers walked through the streets of Manhattan with the graduating students to St. Patrick's Cathedral. At St. Patrick's, we had the graduation ceremony. I felt proud of the students and proud of myself. Given my past circumstances, I was always reminded of the achievements I had made in my own life.

Losing My Job at Cathedral High School

Before my ninth year began, Sister Elizabeth, the dean of studies, called me into her office to ask if there was another subject I could teach. I told her I could probably teach health. I had a deep commitment to my own health and well-being. I believed it was a topic I could be successful with.

It never dawned on me that I would not get a contract for the following school year. I did teach two classes of health in the science department and the other three in the religion department. I also started a stretching class after school. The students enjoyed it, and so did I.

Teachers were called into a conference one day, and the principal explained that due to low student enrollment, the last teacher hired from each department would have to be dismissed. I never thought it was a possibility that I would not receive a contract the following year. I completed my master's degree in theology at St. John's in 1989. At that time, I also received tenure. I needed one more year to receive a pension. Not receiving a contract for the 1992–1993 school year was heartbreaking. I could not believe it. When we received our contracts that Friday afternoon in April, I did not get a contract due to low student enrollment.

Finally, I just decided that it was supposed to be this way. My disappointment was with God. I actually felt devastated. I loved my job and believed I was good at it. I was always acknowledged for the work I did, yet none of it mattered.

It was a difficult time for me. I had just moved into my own apartment at 355 East 61st Street, New York City. I was excited to be only five short blocks from school. This would have been the first time for me to have an easy commute.

I felt depressed over this and decided to put myself back into therapy. I needed to deal with this deep disappointment. I had a job I loved, and through no fault of my own, I was dismissed. I assumed now that I had received tenure, I could not be dismissed. But obviously it was not the case. Finally, I had to accept that it wasn't God's fault and believe that something better would come along. I had to trust, even when I struggled with understanding.

I wondered what was next for me. I was in a bad place emotionally. I loved my apartment and decided I was supposed to be there, even though I would not be teaching five blocks away. I received my paycheck until the end of the summer. I took the summer off to pray about what I was supposed to do with my life next.

Chapter 25

I always had some sort of part-time job when I worked at Cathedral High School. One of the jobs I had was inputting statistics for a friend. He was a political consultant for Senator Roy Goodman, a liberal Republican state senator for over thirty-four years for the Upper East Side of Manhattan. When I lost my job, Joseph advocated for me, and Senator Goodman hired me. I knew that this would not be my life's work, but I needed a job, and he gave me one. I enjoyed working in politics. It was new for me, and I met some really wonderful, caring elected officials.

The Republican Headquarters, NYC

My main job was to maintain the database for thousands of contributors and volunteers. Sometimes I would be asked to type a letter for one of the elected officials. I met Rose, who was the receptionist at the office. She was always willing to lend a hand. She was and is a wonderful person. We have been friends for years and are still friends today. Once, I helped to campaign for the reelection of Senator Roy Goodman, and he told me I was "a campaigner's dream." It was a tremendous amount of fun. Senator Goodman was an excellent public servant, and it was a privilege to work for him.

While working at the Republican headquarters, I often thought about what career was next for me. At one point, I remembered that when I took courses at Baruch College, I had thoughts that I would be a good social worker. At this time, I realized that being a social worker would be a good fit for me to put my faith into action and make a difference.

I decided to apply to Fordham University for a master's in social work. I had to write several papers as to why I thought I should be accepted into the program. I worked hard at sharing all my reasons. My biggest concern was my ability to pay for school. I was always responsible around money and couldn't imagine paying thousands of dollars in school loans. I decided to trust myself that I would figure out a way.

Being Accepted to the Social Work Program

The day I received the letter that I was accepted into the master's program for social work at Fordham University, I felt excited and proud for doing whatever it took to enroll and for not giving up. The master's program was on Saturdays and took three years to complete. Being invited to be in the program was a huge accomplishment. I planned to begin in September 1995.

Blessed to Be Offered a Job at the State Office

Shortly after receiving a raise at the Republican headquarters, everything changed. Senator Goodman had to reduce his staff. He called me into his office and offered me a position at his state office as his receptionist, and I accepted. It was a blessing that he had an opening at his state office, or I would have been out of a job.

I took calls from elderly constituents who needed a listening ear. I also had the opportunity to learn a tremendous amount of information about policy and legislation, rent control laws, and various other topics that are important to constituents. I enjoyed my job but knew eventually I would be attending graduate school for social work. I hoped it would all work out.

All during my time at Senator Goodman's office, Mother was in and out of hospitals. I made every effort to visit her whenever I could.

Chapter 26

I deeply loved my mother. I had compassion for her pain. The last couple of years of her life, she was totally dependent on me for emotional support. She and I became closer than we had ever been. I knew when the time came for her to leave this world, it would be difficult for me to let go.

My sisters Annie and June did not live in New York City. They moved to Florida several years earlier. My younger sister Connie, her four children, and boyfriend lived with Mother for eight years. One day in 1990, they all moved out, and Mother was alone. I was left to take responsibility for her. I had lived with Mother for only eight years during my youth. It was not until the last fifteen years of her life that I grew to care about her well-being.

My sister Annie paid all Mother's bills from Florida. I took on the responsibility of handling her many medical needs. She went to the hospital for many conditions, such as eye surgery, diabetes, emphysema, heart disease, senile dementia, and rectal cancer.

The last couple of years, I'd grown to love Mother more. When she went into the hospital, I tried to visit her often. It was time-consuming and never easy. She was often placed in a Brooklyn hospital.

During this time, Mother told me that she wished she had allowed herself to know me years ago and that she thought I was such a beautiful person.

Since Connie and her children had moved out of Mother's apartment, she became unhappy about her living situation.

Mother was in the hospital often the last several years of her life. Since she had Medicaid, she was often sent home from the hospital and provided with home attendants, visiting nurses, and social workers who came to the house. At first, she had a home attendant for eight hours, then twenty-four hours, and then finally two twelve-hour shifts. She was constantly falling and had medical problems that caused her to be in and out of the hospital.

Whenever Mother was at the hospital, I made every effort to be in communication with the social worker. I often gave him or her the information for Mom's providers. Several times, especially if Mom's floor was changed, a discharge was done in such a rush that the providers were not informed of Mother's return home. It always frightened me when that happened.

While Mom was in the hospital for a heart problem, I worked with the social worker on the ninth floor who took an interest in her. Mother really liked her. She said later, "My friend came to see me again. She asked me how I was feeling."

Mother felt special and important whenever the social worker visited with her. At times, I depended on the social workers for advice. Oftentimes, I felt overwhelmed by all the responsibility.

Another time, I went to visit Mother and she was unconscious for several days. I was asked for permission to insert a feeding tube in her for nourishment. I was told if they put the tube in, it would be permanent. I asked for another day to pray about it. The next day, Mother became conscious again, and it wasn't necessary.

One time toward the end, when Mother was in the hospital, she went in for one thing, and they found out she had a tumor in her rectum. She had surgery for the tumor and radiation treatments that left her with constant diarrhea.

I often talked to Mother about going into a nursing home, and she would get extremely upset. She became verbally abusive. I had to calm her down and let it go. Eventually, she had no choice. The hospital refused to send her home.

Mother's health was failing. I realized that I needed to find a nursing home close to where I lived. I began working with the Mary Manning Walsh Nursing Home in Manhattan. I was told it was one of the finest nursing homes in New York. I went for the initial interview and was given lots of forms to fill out. I started the process.

The next day, when I arrived at the hospital, I discovered that they had moved Mother to another floor. She was confused and disoriented. She was very sick. I tried to speak to the social worker from the ninth floor and was told she was no longer on Mother's case.

The next day, I received a phone call at work from a social worker who took over my mother's case. She informed me that she was confirming the plan for a nursing home. I explained that Mother could only be placed at Mary Manning Walsh. Any other placement was unacceptable.

When I met the social worker the next afternoon, she explained the procedure. I had to pick three nursing homes, and if none of them agreed to take Mother, she would automatically be placed in any nursing home near the hospital. I said, "I am unwilling for this to happen. I picked Mary Manning Walsh." I had been in communication with Mary Manning Walsh and had most of Mom's paperwork completed.

Sad News

A few days later, the social worker called to inform me that Mary Manning Walsh said there were five people on the waiting list, and she thought it would be impossible to get Mother into this facility. I asked her to give me a little more time. She agreed.

A Miracle Achieved for Mother

When I hung up the phone, I cried and cried. Then I reminded myself that I never give up, and I was not going to give up now.

It meant too much to me. I took powerful, committed action and swallowed my pride and embarrassment and asked for help.

Since I had taught at Cathedral High School for nine years, I called Sister Elizabeth, the dean of studies. I asked her to advocate for Mother, and she agreed. She wrote a letter on Mother's behalf.

Chares Mallard was an elected official in New York City in 1994. He was an incredible person. He was an attorney and a former VISTA volunteer. I reached out to him because I felt confident, he would advocate for Mother, and he did.

I then looked at how important it was for my mother to be accepted into Mary Manning Walsh. I decided I felt brave enough to make an appointment to speak with Senator Goodman. I told him the whole story. He had a lot of respect for me for the work I did for him, and he was totally willing to have his chief of staff call Mary Manning Walsh on his behalf.

The next day, after Senator Goodman put in the call, I received a phone call at work from Mary Manning Walsh. I was told that if I was willing to pay one day for my mother's bed and could get her there the next day, there was a bed waiting for her. I had a feeling of pleasure and satisfaction that I was willing to do whatever it took to have this miracle happen.

I took care of everything I needed to do to have Mother transferred to Mary Manning Walsh the next day. Senator Goodman gave me the following day off to be with Mother at her new home. She was disoriented and upset. She did not want to be in a nursing home. She wanted me to take her home. I tried to explain that she had no choice. She needed the care.

I finally had to promise Mother that if she got better, I would take her home. I knew she would never go home, but she needed to believe it was possible, so I let her. Whenever I had a conversation about her being in the nursing home because she couldn't take care of herself, she got extremely angry and demanded I take her home. She refused to stay in her room and insisted I pack her bags.

My mother kept falling, and she realized she wasn't getting any better. She became depressed and withdrawn. I knew how lonely and unhappy she felt in the nursing home, and there was nothing I could do, except be there for her and try to bring her some joy.

Eventually, she was beginning to accept the nursing home a little more. She had a crush on the male nurse who took care of her, and it gave her something positive to put her attention on.

I visited Mother at least five times a week. The nursing home was walking distance from my apartment, which made it easier to be with her.

On Sunday morning, I took Mother to Mass at the Catholic church in the nursing home. After church, we had breakfast in the cafeteria, and then I wheeled her upstairs.

Mother lived successfully for five months at the nursing home. We both were beginning to enjoy each other. I was aware she had senile dementia. It wasn't funny, but she would make me laugh. She would tell me not to use a certain exit when I left to go home. There was a boogeyman waiting at the exit. I often listened and went through the exit she requested as I laughed to myself.

St. Vincent's Hospital

One day while I was at work, I received a call from Mary Manning Walsh reporting that Mother had been taken to St. Vincent's Hospital. On her own, Mother had tried to get up from her wheelchair to go to the bathroom, and she fell and broke her hip.

I went directly to the hospital. It was Friday afternoon, and by the time she was admitted with paperwork and all, it was after 5:00 p.m. It was upsetting. Mother was in excruciating pain. It was so bad that even with the pain medication they gave her, she suffered. I stayed with her until I had to leave after 8:00 p.m. I returned the next day, and she was still in pain. They said they couldn't operate until they had received all her records and taken other tests, so she had to wait until Monday. I felt so bad for her. I sat there with her as she just moaned in pain, and all I could do was hold her hand.

The next day was Sunday, and I visited Mother for a few hours. When I was leaving, she said, "Ruthie, I love you."

And I said, "Mommy, I love you."

Around three o'clock Monday morning, I received a phone call from St. Vincent's Hospital. The doctor wanted my consent to place Mother on a machine for her heart.

I had no idea what to say. I asked, "Doctor, if it were your mother, would you put her on the machine?"

He said, "Yes."

I asked if I needed to get down to the hospital as soon as possible.

He said, "Ruth, you can wait until the morning. Your mother should be fine."

I went to the hospital around 8:00 a.m. on November 14, 1994. The hospital staff had me wait downstairs when I asked for a pass. I had no idea why. I thought maybe they were having a shift change.

Finally, the nurse said I could go upstairs.

When I got to my mother's room, there was a doctor sitting outside. He told me that Mother had passed away.

I couldn't believe my ears. I was in shock. I called my nephew Tommy, and he handled everything. He told my sisters Annie and June. They were both in Florida, so they were able to be together.

The hospital allowed me to be with Mother for over an hour. I sat there with deep grief. I was torn to pieces. I remembered how our last words spoken to each other were "I love you." It was all I had ever wanted to hear from her. I held her hand and touched her, telling her how much I loved her and that I would miss her forever.

For a while after Mother died, I would wake up in the middle of the night crying. The realization that I would never see her again was difficult to accept.

During my lifetime, I have attended many workshops. Often at some point in the workshop, we were asked to write letters to our parents. I would like to share several letters I wrote to Mother but never gave to her.

Letter #1

Dear Mommy,

I am writing to you even though I know you are never going to read this since you cannot see well enough, nor would you be able to fully understand.

My whole life has been structured around wanting and needing your love. In my thirties, I realized the way to get your love was to stop expecting it but instead give it, and it seemed to work. As the years went on, I learned how to forgive you for leaving me when I was three years old and for rarely finding time for me when you left me in the orphanage. You picked Annie to go home for a weekend visit instead of me, your baby. You rarely showed me love and rarely listened to me. You often were manipulative and unkind toward me to get what you wanted. For most of my teenage years, I thought I hated you, and for most of my life, I didn't particularly like your personality and your ways of relating.

As I said before, when I was in my thirties, I learned to forgive you. But I also noticed I didn't spend a whole lot of time around you. I called you maybe once a week and only visited you on holidays and your birthday. But one thing for sure, when I did visit you, it was to bring you joy. I would buy you gifts and take you out to dinner. I probably could count on one hand how many times you called me until the end when you needed me. I never remember you calling me when I was married to Paul. Yet, he and I often took you out for dinner.

In the Forum in 1989, I shared something you said to me that made a huge contribution to my life, and Werner Erhard also acknowledged you for your bigness. It was the birthday I gave you one hundred dollars for something you wanted, bought you a dress, and was taking you out for dinner. You looked at me and said, "I never did anything for you your whole life, and you are so good to me. I don't deserve it." Mom, I was so proud of you for being so honest, and it was at that point that I was finally able to admire and respect you.

In the last two years, Mommy, everything changed. Every time you were in the hospital, I came to see you and be there for you. You knew you could count on me. Then Connie and all her kids moved out of your apartment and left you all by yourself. I began visiting you consistently once or twice a week. You structured your whole weekend around my visit. At first, I was able to handle it, as I was making a huge contribution to you, and I was loving it. Then I started getting daily phone calls from you. You became attached to me to the point of needing me.

I am constantly struggling with your neediness. Sometimes I feel trapped because I don't know how to help you, or I don't want to help you, or I want one of your other daughters to share in the responsibility, especially since they all lived with you and I didn't, which is always my justification for not wanting to handle all your problems. Love, Ruthie

Letter #2

Dear Mommy,

I must admit on some level I have become very attached to you this past year. You call me all the time, several times a day. I know how lonely you are and how rejected you feel by your other children. I was almost the only one who visited you often for a year when you were in and out of the hospital. You know you can count on me whenever you need or want anything, but when you complain constantly, I cannot handle it. Also, when you are abusive to the home attendants, I get very upset.

Sometimes I feel guilty for wanting to put you into a nursing home. The guilt is that part of me that wants to do it so I don't have to deal with you so intimately every day. I don't have to hear your constant complaints. But another part of me feels you would be much happier since you would not be so alone. Except, then I think that you are always upset over something and never seem happy, and since you have a point of view of not wanting to live in a nursing home, you would probably hate it there too.

I wish you would look for things you have to be thankful for in life and find some joy, but that is a rare case with you. Sometimes I think that if you had one of your other daughters by your side, I would think nothing of only seeing you on holidays and your birthday and call you once a week instead of every day.

When I think of leaving New York, I feel trapped by you. I feel I cannot leave and abandon you. Then I get angry because I think, *Why me?* Why not one of the daughters you always loved more than me?

Lately, I have been so concerned for your well-being since you keep falling. Also, since you are having problems keeping a home attendant because of your unmanageable behavior. I wonder if I am doing you a disservice by not putting you in a nursing home, as much as you don't want to go.

Mommy, in spite of all my mixed feelings, you know I love you deeply, and I know you love me. What I want is to be able to contribute to you freely, so I make a difference in your life without all the effort and struggle I add to it. I am committed to not abandoning you and to always being there for you no matter what happens, but I pray I will make the right choices, so you do not hurt yourself and have as many years as possible left to live. I want to visit you out of contribution instead of feeling you're a hassle or that I have to fit you in my tight schedule all the time. I am going to do something special for you for your birthday next week. Love, Ruthie

Letter #3

Dear Mommy,

I love you very much, and I am so happy that I get the opportunity to tell you every day. Last night, I wrote this four-page letter going on and on about the past, and when I read it today, I was ashamed of myself.

I am so happy that I have this opportunity to realize how selfish I am when it comes to you. I said

I forgive you for the past, but I lied. In everything I do for you, what is in the background is that I owe you nothing. Tonight, I realized how much I really do owe you. You gave me life, and that is the best gift anyone could give. If it weren't for you, I wouldn't be the beautiful person I am. I promise from now on to be committed to give myself to you from contribution and not burden. I am going to look at the time I spend with you as an opportunity to love you. Mommy, I never took the time to put myself in your shoes. Now, doing that even for a couple of minutes, I am so sorry for how difficult life is for you. Instead of holding you as a burden, I want to thank you for trusting me to take care of you.

It must be so difficult with all those medical problems you have. Your poor eyesight, your heart disease, then you end up with cancer of the rectum and had to go through radiation treatments. You never get visitors; no wonder you are so lonely all the time. As the years go on and I realize how little life really gave you, I feel sorry for you. I did many workshops and learned to love you unconditionally.

Mommy, I forgive you for everything you did when I was little, and I honor the last couple of years that we have had a great, loving, forgiving relationship.

Love, Ruthie

Printed in the United States
by Baker & Taylor Publisher Services